A Lad from Brantford
& other essays

By DAVID ADAMS RICHARDS

Small Heroics (poetry) 1972
The Coming of Winter 1974
Blood Ties 1976
Dancers at Night (short stories) 1978
Lives of Short Duration 1981
Road to the Stilt House 1985
Nights Below Station Street 1988
Evening Snow will Bring Such Peace 1990
For Those Who Hunt the Wounded Down 1993
A Lad From Brantford & other essays 1994

DAVID ADAMS RICHARDS

A Lad From Brantford
& other essays

Broken Jaw Press
Fredericton • Canada

Acknowledgements:
Several of these essays have previously been published in *Chatelaine, FREE Magazine, The Globe and Mail, The New Brunswick Reader Magazine, New Muse of Contempt, Writing Away: The PEN Canada Travel Anthology* (McClelland & Stewart, 1994), and broadcast on *Information Morning* (CBC Radio).

Published by Broken Jaw Press.
Cover design by Karin Sundin.
Cover art: detail from "Hanging by a Thread," 24" x 36", egg tempra, 1994, by William Forrestall, from the collection of Jane Taylor. Photographed by Geoffrey Gammon. Reproduced by permission of the artist.
Author photo by Martin Flewwelling.
Book design by Joe Blades.

First edition
Printed and bound in Canada
10 9 8 7 6 5 4 3 2 1

Canadian Cataloguing in Publication Data
Richards, David Adams, 1950-

    A lad from Brantford, and other essays

    ISBN 0-921411-25-1

I. Title.

PS8585.I17L33 1994   C814´.54   C94-950231-6
PR9199.3.R53L33 1994

Broken Jaw Press
M•A•P•Productions
Box 596 Stn A
Fredericton NB E3B 5A6
Canada

A Lad From Brantford
& other essays

A Lad from Brantford

A lad from Brantford once said to me: "We all think of you guys as real stupid, ignorant of the country—but you got dope and murder down there too."

He was not making such an unusual statement. The Roman poet Juvenal made it as well when he suggested that only country bumpkins could possibly be displeased any longer with adultery.

The idea both of them had, 2000 years apart, was that cosmopolitan advantage is mirrored through vice: a vice which no rural sensibility is sophisticated enough to understand.

Sophisticated is the key word here.

Conversely to this idea, (and yet working from the same principle) is the one popularized by dozens and dozens of movies over the last 30 years. It is the idea that vice in rural areas is something which most people are superior to. Vice in rural areas comes from backward and repressive mentalities. It is inferior vice. It does not belong to the great, almost liberating category of vice in Los Angeles—there is something unpleasantly vulgar about rural vice. We always run white lightening instead of cocaine.

In these movies, of which I have seen most, there is always something sinister about leaving the safety of the big city to travel into the rural areas. Someone never wants to go. This hesitation is a warning to us, which only those on the trip fail to recognize.

Because, for millions of people, rural life is a bogeyman waiting to happen.

As the wife of the doctor in *Arachnophobia*, a horror movie about a bunch of spiders, that I saw a few years back, says—she will have to give up caffeine and office politics if she goes to a small town.

Of course, how could there ever be office politics in a town of under 1.5 million—or more subtly, how could a fashionable woman be involved in it, if the town is so small? Who would take a chance and hire her?

These movies almost always work on this derogatory premise. Which is about as self-congratulatory to a one-sided view as you can get. Also, we find from many of these movies that there is no neutrality in a small town. Most dislike the urban newcomers because their ideas are "newfangled." We are supposed to wink and give wry smiles.

Well, they are distrusted, except by the one educated person in every movie about every small town who always lives alone, has taken a course and who wants to get away.

For instance, in *Arachnophobia*, no one will dare go to a new doctor who graduated from a famous university and comes from a large city, because of inbred rural fear and suspicion. Except of course for one enlightened woman. Everyone is suspicious of the university degree.

In these movies, country people are always suspicious of learning. And learning is always university learning.

The actual learning of physical life and labour, is either shown as sinister or hokey. If a man uses a thresher, you know he's looking to mince your bones, especially if you've just flown in from New York.

In dozens of movies where the urbans meet the rurals, rural people never stare long and hard, they stare at you and drool.

And it follows that in *Arachnophobia*, a young girl from the town going to university in a big city is going to major in "gym." Moronic attitudes are always in fashion in small towns.

No wonder the lad from Brantford said what he did. It was only natural. It was the only way he knew his country—watching American movies.

And in these movies the ideas presented are simply assumed as true because they come from an urban viewpoint.

The one insistent idea is that the language and culture of modern men and women is unknown in rural areas by rural people.

And this is the undergirded message about the evil of rural life. It's not that rural people have vice or even that they murder or rape. But that they murder and rape because they oppose the principals of progress, and don't know what big words mean.

Rural people often don't understand words. Words like nepotism—in *Arachnophobia*, people at the town picnic think it is a religion. Or autistic; in *The Rainman*, the small town nurse thinks Tom Cruise says "artistic."

All this is well and fine. But the subliminal suggestion is that this mistake is a rural one, and as such is always set up to amuse us.

We, who live in or near rural areas, have been fed this for decades, and will continue to be. It's just a matter of going along with it, like riding the rails, on a train that don't belong to you.

These movies show rural life and law everywhere *being* fascist towards women and minorities, brutal toward animals on the verge of extinction.

And it always takes the main actor or actress down from the North to straighten out the evil of a small town in Georgia, or up from New York to save the whales in Newfoundland.

Not that there are no bigoted sheriffs in Georgia. But one would assume from watching movies like *Macon County Line* that what is bigoted, and what is not, is absolutely clarified by the people and police from L.A.

People from cities have had a phobia about rural life for generations. And it is so ingrained in hundreds upon hundreds of movies that Canadians from urban centres hope to prove that they too are an urban society. Smelt sheds are out. Condo sharing is in. Many of us worry if our country will ever be mentioned in a movie, and how will we be represented.

And we do our own movies. Like *Labour of Love*. I don't know if anyone remembers it. This is a movie made some years ago, where the troubleshooter from the union comes down from Toronto to settle a dispute in the backwater of the Miramichi.

They dress and talk like loose cannon out of Toronto's idea of the Deep South of 70 years ago in this movie made in 1984.

For instance, the women wear bib overalls and wash for 11 or 12 children, (large families always show ignorance of forethought) and the men think it funny if someone runs about in his underwear—of course they don't know he's jogging.

But there is a more serious underlying message here. There always is in these things.

In *Labour of Love*, it is the idea that there must be entrenched values in places like the Miramichi, or the upper Saint John River, or the Humber in Newfoundland, or anywhere else, and therefore these values must be wrong. So the bib overalls show where such value lies. The smirk is about tradition, the backdrop is country bumpkin.

But *Labour of Love* is not really a Canadian movie— because nothing about Canada is known to the people who made it.

Nor did they know which formula to follow. The movie *Labour of Love* is half-British *Carry On...* gang and half-American *Gomer Pile*.

Yet all the trends of *Arachnophobia* are followed in it. A pregnant woman wearing coveralls is gap-toothed and backward, whereas the only intelligent woman, who has wonderful teeth, wants to leave the town before she too has to devote her life to child-bearing and "splitting cod."

And, to prove her worth, she goes swimming nude.

We all get a good laugh over this because of how the simplistic fishermen who see her react. (Fall out of their boats.)

I'm almost certain that bathing in the nude is frowned upon in Toronto parks more than it ever was at Oak Point, New Brunswick, but it must be for a different reason.

And of course it is for a different reason. In a movie about Toronto, female nakedness might be considered exploitive. Upon the Miramichi it is such a startling revelation (that a pretty girl would bare her breasts) that it has to be considered at least irreverent, even liberating.

Also, I believe in my heart that, consciously or not, none of this is innocent fun but a base set-up of criteria upon which to value life.

Children are bad, pregnancy is often wrong, and rural life offers you both. More than enough of these and not much of anything else.

In its own way, *Labour of Love* is emulating the Deep South movies of a decade and a half ago.

But the redeeming feature of movies like *Macon County Line* is that they had some car chases and blood and guts.

We rarely have that in Canada. A Canadian sex movie will have almost everything except the sex, and I swear to God, I once saw a Canadian monster picture where no one ever got to see a monster.

Even a little one.

The lad from Brantford can be forgiven. Like the 13th century shoemaker who pointed toward the sea and said to his son:

"There be dragons."

He just repeated what he'd been told.

—1988

My Old Newcastle

We all played on the ice floes in the spring, spearing tommy cod with stolen forks tied to sticks. And more than one of us almost met our end slipping off the ice when we were seven and eight.

All night, the trains rumbled, and shunted their loads off to Halifax or Montreal, and the men moved and worked. And to this day, I find the sound of trains more comforting than lonesome. It was somehow thrilling to know of people up and about at those hours, and of wondrous events taking place. Always somehow with the faint worn smell of gas and steel.

This is a great working river.

There was always the presence of working men and women, from the mines or mills or woods, the more-than-constant sound of machinery, and ore covered in tarps at the side of the wharf.

But, as children, we all saw movies on Saturday afternoons—sitting in our snowsuits and hats and heavy boots—that had nothing to do with us—in fact, that never mentioned us as a country or a place. That never seemed to know what our fathers and mothers did—that we went to wars or had a flag or even a great passion for life.

As far as the movies were concerned, we were in a lost dark country, it seemed. And perhaps this is one reason I write. Leaving the theatre on a January afternoon, the smell of worn seats and heat and chip bags gave way to a muted cold and a scent of snow no movie ever showed us. And night came against the tin roofs of the sheds behind our white houses, as the long spires of our churches rose over the town.

Our river was frozen so blue then, that trucks could travel from one town to the other across the ice, and bonfires were lit by kids skating, sparks rising from the shore, under the stars, as mothers called children home at nine o'clock.

All winder long the sky was tinted blue on the horizon, the schools we sat in too warm. Privileged boys and girls sat beside those who lived in hunger and constant worry. One went on to be a Rhodes scholar, another was a derelict at 17 and dead at 20. To this day I could not tell you which held more promise.

Spring came with the smell of mud and grass burning in the fields above us. Road hockey gave way to cricket and then baseball. The sun warmed, the ice shifted, and then the river was free. Salmon and sea trout moved up a dozen of our tributaries to spawn.

In summer, the ships came in, from all ports to ours, to carry ore and paper away. Sailors smoked black tobacco cigarettes staring down at us from their decks; black flies spoiled in the fields beyond town and the sky was large all evening. Cars filled with children too excited to sleep passed along our great avenues lines with overhanging trees. All down to the store to get ice cream in the dark.

Adolescent blueberry crops and sunken barns dotted the fields near the bay, where the air had the taste of salt and tar, and seemed constantly filled with wind where, by August, the water shimmered and even the small white lobster boats smelled of autumn, as did the ripples that moved them.

In the autumn, the leaves were red, of course, and the earth, by Thanksgiving, became as hard as a dull turnip. Ice formed in the ditches and shallow streams. The fields became yellow and stiff. The sounds of rifle shots from men deer hunting echoed faintly away, while women walked in kerchiefs and coats to seven o'clock mass, and the air felt heavy and leaden. Winter coming on again.

Now the town is three times as large, and fast food franchises and malls dot the roadside where there were once fields and lumber yards. There is a new process at the mill, and much of the wood is clearcut, so that huge areas lie empty and desolate—a redundancy of broken and muted earth. The river is opened all winter by an ice breaker, so no trucks can travel across the ice, and the trains, of course, are gone—for the most part, the station is empty, the tracks fiercely alone in the winter sun.

The theatre is gone now too. And those thousands of movies showing us, as children filled with happy laughter someplace in Canada, what we were not, are gone as well. Given way to videos and satellite dishes, and a community that is growing slowly farther and farther away from its centre. Neither bad nor good, I suppose—but away from what it was.

—1988

Children

Sometimes the more institutionalized the reason for a picture of children, the more it shows the children whole enough to accept their fate.

A parade up a church aisle long ago, for First Communion, or an exhibit of photographs about orphanages in London, England, in the 1880s, before those small orphans, the Home Children, entered ships to be sent off to Canada and Australia.

Little Emma Cook, age four, holding a second-hand doll, on her way to Canada. Or a five-year-old named Tom, with one leg missing, standing on crutches, smiling, as if someone had just revealed to him that he would be sent off alone to Australia and he said: "Australia, sure."

When St. Paul spoke about enduring all things, he spoke about children.

And when he spoke of hoping for all things, he spoke of children.

Any Kool-Aid stand will tell you that.

Perhaps no one could imagine how hard Jack London worked when he was a child.

Or cared, really, except as a way to change the laws.

The one thing children rarely exhibit are the self-righteous opinions that pretend to come on their behalf.

Joe Louis at one time took on the work of the other boys around him because he know they were not strong enough to do it: moving crates and ice blocks, at 11 years of age, up tenement stairs.

Many of my uncles and my wife's uncles worked in the woods from the time they were 12 and 13, and took home less money in a day than you or I would now pay for a cup of coffee.

And one of the poorest boys I knew went to work for two years in order to get enough money so both he and his brother could start university together.

The practice of the chimney sweep that William Blake wrote about is long past, where little boys of five and six were known to have smothered inside chimneys they were cleaning.

But at least some of the opinions of our day are probably as intellectually deceitful as the kind that allowed chimney sweeps, or, for that matter, allowed boatloads of orphans like Emma Cook to be sent here from England in the 1880s. And come from the same mentality. It is what Dickens' fictional Oliver Twist had to face growing up in the 1830s—the demagogy of an adjustable social program. A program that is always scaled for people we consider beneath us, but which we refuse to admit we consider beneath us.

Children have often been used as poker chips in the game of self-seeking, so much so that even the pictures of starving children create a degree of cynicism that no new diet fad could match. And allow us to vent our arguments against the children themselves.

Most of my friends, especially those of university background, believe it only appropriate and considerate not to want children, except under the right conditions.

And let's face it, this is thought to be a radically new concept. (Supposedly, people like Princess Hélène in Tolstoy's *War and Peace* could not have thought like this.)

For instance, I have not been to a dinner party in the last 12 to 15 years (no matter what organized religion, in no matter what region of the province) where the topic of unwanted children as a terrible problem did not come up. Usually sanctimoniously, or pejoratively; usually half-way through the meal.

Although what was camouflaged is the fact that when you talk of children as a problem, the last thing you are doing is taking the child's side.

Yet at these parties the arguement is that we are now, as never before, a very sensitive people who find it inexcusable how the world treats children, so it is best not to have many of them around.

And I am always left thinking of at least some of the children I knew—the 11 children whose dad was a fireman and was killed fighting a fire in 1955, or those other boys and girls, in the far-off time off the 1950s, waiting at the back door of the bakery, in winter, to get a piece of bread before they went to school.

Little Emma Cook boarding a ship with a second-hand doll to travel to New Brunswick in 1884 because someone somewhere thought that she was a problem that could be solved.

And I think of this at the dinner party when we talk.

It is also interesting, to me, to note the pretension of these dinner party views in the face of people who are unable to have children. People who cannot have children of their own are often looked upon with the rather comic artificial sympathy they always were.

Just as my mother was looked upon with such sympathy, that didn't even care to hide that it was false, because she had six children.

A professor once suggested kindly that my mother was a victim because she had a large family. He was shocked that I would of one moment hesitate to agree. It was not because of what he said that made me disagree, but the inference he wished his remark to betray.

The inference was, that my mother was never educated enough to make up her own mind, and couldn't, anyway, being as she was, a woman of the 40s and '50s.

Which made her exactly what he considered her, being less than himself.

And as an afterthought he told me in a whisper, something he assumed I did not know, that children suffered too.

His reasoning concurs, if Emma Cook, holding the second-hand doll in 1884, ready to get on a ship to Canada, had not been born she would not have suffered. As if anyone could guarantee the degree of suffering of any human being, even himself.

To me, nothing is less compassionate, more blinkered, and more smugly self-assured than this view.

I've also found that the stereotype that most dinner party conversations exhibit about the parents of large families is no better than the ones detergent commercials had of women in the '50s.

The bare bones of their argument has always struck me as this: that there should be a proper economic and intellectual table for being born that will forego our need for charity, and moreover, there should be some way to implement this condition.

A condition that would neglect a good many of the friends I value and probably myself. And most assuredly, many of the people that spout the argument.

It's kind of similar to the principled upper classes, a century and a half ago, considering the poor as not human. Let's say, about the time William Blake was writing his *Songs of Innocence and of Experience*, or earlier still, when Jonathan Swift was writing "A Modest Proposal."

I don't even think little Emma Cook would have given one second of her life for the casual opinion the professor had about her birth. Nor do I think that her suffering was not bountiful and filled with the same hope as his own children's.

What we really don't want is any more little Emma Cooks. In a way, it comes from a misguided noble sentiment: we do not wish humanity to suffer as we know she did.

If this is the sentiment, then the expedient measure is not to give her a chance at it. Cutting the head off a problem is one sure way to handle it. Setting her adrift on a ship to Canada is another.

The whole idea is that thinking this way is a psychic act of self-sacrifice on our part at the dinner party.

Rather like the portly overseer of some social program of the mid-1880s.

But one should never be the recipient of a benefit from one's own altruism, to the receiver of that altruism's debt.

I'm only saying this: It's fine, altogether, not to want something, or to never want it for others either. But don't let us pretend it's because we care for it, or them. The ignorant, or young, or poverty-stricken, who have too many children, included.

The real notes of hope come from the children themselves. Not those who garner them a problem. Come from Emma Cook, wherever that ship took her.

The doubters are always ourselves.

Years and years ago, on the Miramichi, a tiny seven-year-old girl jumped off a dory into the bay to save her five-year-old brother. In spite of her courage she was unable to bring him to safety.

When a diver found the bodies some time later, they were sitting upright in the sand on the bottom, holding hands.

I've never heard dinner party concern about children, yet, that even comes close to such wisdom.

—1991

Smoking

I began to smoke at the age of three, with my friend
Kenny, under the veranda of his house, about the autumn
of 1954.

We would crawl behind the steps, squeeze our way
under the veranda, and light up our first cigarette of the
day—which was ten minutes after our mothers had
scrubbed and dressed us, fed us, and threw us outside for
the morning.

All of this happened years ago, and my memories of
children are faint and distant; and are, that they were
always dressed in some bright colours as they walked
along the paths between our small white houses.

There was always the smell of wood and smoke at
night, and the smell of earth. There were ships in at the
wharf, and old men still wore Humphrey pants.
Sometimes they had a good pair of Humphrey pants along
with a regular work pair. The women wore long dresses
and some had a mink collar on their winter coats. The
radios were still as large as one livingroom wall: T.V.'s
were a rare commodity.

Kenny's mother's purse, black and aristocratic looking,
sat upon the counter, with its package of Export sticking
out the top of it: sunlight coming through those old
venetian blinds in the corner.

The one thing about thieves I know, is that when I knew most of them they were young enough to have a sense of hilarity about their vocation. Gain was nothing without the hilarity attached to it.

As soon as his mother began to clean the house, Kenny would go after those cigarettes with a bravery most people only admire from a distance.

I suppose today he might be called slightly hyperactive. We would be out the door and under the veranda and lighting up. We would sit back against the blackened brick foundation, and stare at the floor of the veranda—puffs of smoke seeping through the cracks in the boards—and look through the lattice work, to watch my grandmother come around to the coal chute, or watch the milkman standing on the veranda above us, wisps of smoke about his feet.

Years have passed, and you know, almost half of the children I grew up with are gone: booze in cars going too fast in the night, or some other sad assault upon the body. Those brilliant and wonderful children that I still see in old photos, standing in the school yards in the snow.

No cigarette has ever tasted better than the ones I had when I was three and four. The smell of tobacco in the tight paper, mingling with the smell of autumn burdocks scraping the side of the wall in the cooling wind—was I suppose as close to purity as I will ever be.

The trouble was Kenny didn't think so.

It is a fact of my life that I have often been close to people who will NEVER EVER leave well enough alone—but who, for some peculiar reason, have to continually TEMPT God. And worse still, bring me along—as in this instance, as a sort of burnt offering.

It isn't that he lit me on fire, right away—but I did notice him becoming more and more remote—as if he were drawn to some other purpose his mere two-and-one-half-foot best friend in the world couldn't comprehend.

And never minding all the times he reprimanded me for letting too much smoke go out through the slats, or squeeze up through the boards and rise toward the milkman's knees, he suddenly took it into his head, to smoke on the street by the pole—leaning up against it, just once, like the adults did, with our ankles crossed.

So one morning that's what we did. We walked out of our hiding place, with fresh cigarettes in our gobs, like tiny Humphrey Bogarts, and walked right into the arms of my aunt who was coming down the sidewalk.

"Is that a cigarette?"

(I shook my head NO—as if it wasn't a cigarette)

"MY good GOD," she said. "I'm telling your mother."

"She knows I smoke," I said.

This was the first of two or three sentences my aunt and I ever exchanged.

Of course I lied. I had not really told my mother yet. And anyway my mother was standing out on the porch at that moment.

I don't think I would have smoked so readily after that day if it weren't for Kenny.

Time passed. We smoked in fields, and when snow fell and made the ground ash white, we smoked behind the fence that separated our property. Long ago, we puffed in the sheds across the street, and sitting in the gully, with cigarettes in our pockets and tucked away in our mittens; and when we couldn't get cigarettes we rolled up newspaper and put leaves in them. And once when we couldn't find a pole to stand beside, we smoked in a hole dug for one, leaned up against the shale rocks and crossed our ankles.

And though we thought we were well-hidden, as children always do, we must have been in plain view to grown-ups half the time—because always we were caught, searched, scolded and forbidden to do it ever again. And they were continually sniffing us up and down—twice a day, at least.

These were the same days as when another little friend of mine jumped off the roof of his house using an umbrella as a parachute, and a young woman—younger then, than I am now by 20 years, had an infant who was dying, and would stop Kenny and I on the street, as if by talking to us she was somehow able to ease her pain. Nor did I ever feel she wanted other adults around when she spoke. But too often we were trying to hide cigarette smoke when she came to see us. And I never knew her name: remember now only one thing, that her soft wavy hair was brown.

But these in truth are my first few unclear memories of what became in a way a lifelong addiction.

(I have finally managed to quit.)

Another memory is the movie.

Kenny and I were staring at Rory Calhoan, and Rory Calhoan was lighting a cigarette off a stick he had taken out of a fire, while he leaned back against his saddlebags after a hard day's ride.

And Kenny came to some conclusions about how we should smoke from then on.

We would go home, he said, and build a fire in his back yard, heat the sticks and light our cigarettes from them. We would, in essence, have a permanent supply of matches.

25 🖎

No one would see the fire, he explained, because we would build it so close to the house—right near the oil barrel—that it would be hidden from view, and we would never let it go out.

Kenny never thought the fire got out of hand, even when my coat sleeve lit up when I was dipping a stick into it. Never once was he daunted in his effort to light a cigarette like a cowboy. Even when he was being hauled away, kicking and screaming, by his mother.

The wall of his house was seared for a year with a burn mark that rose to the kitchen window in the shape of a spruce tree.

The oil barrel was drained and carried to the basement.

Kenny began to carry a silver cigarette case about with him—who knows where he got it: sometimes there were even cigarettes in it. And he began to puff on his father's cigars whenever he could get his hands on one—and invite me over when his parents were out and Charles, his brother, who was supposed to babysit him was playing road hockey.

His mother threatened to send him to a home—where the Jesuits would take over. That was the most common threat in those days.

"I'll send you to a home and let the Jesuits take over." But she never quite had the heart to.

So it was close to Christmas 39 years ago that Kenny lit the couch in his house on fire with a big White Owl cigar. He had crawled behind the couch and had lit it, puffing away solemnly, not realizing that the tip of the cigar was burning against the couch.

He barely escaped alive.

They dragged the couch outside and let it sit in the snow and mud, upside down.

I don't remember Kenny's father very well, but his plan seemed ingenious. He went to the store and came home with a pack of fat White Owls. And then they tied Kenny in his highchair. Then they handed him matches.

"Here you go," his father said. "You little bugger— smoke them all."

It is what was once known as the aversion addiction treatment. An arcane and cruel method of dealing with addicts—and, back in the 1950s, in its infant stages—which is probably just as well.

"See, you'll soon get sick now," his father said, "Smoke them all—you'll see."

They stood about the highchair glaring down at him, while Kenny, in weary compliance, struck his first match.

After awhile the rest of the family sat down to breakfast.

At that moment Kenny's aunt drove into the yard. All the way from Nova Scotia. Came for a Christmas visit and wanting to surprise them. She walked through the door. Everyone happy to see her, the baby nonchalantly flicking the ash from his cigar with an experienced finger.

"My God, Jenny," she said. "I didn't know the baby smoked."

I lost touch with him when I moved to the other end of town. As over the years I have lost touch with so many of those children I knew and grew up with, and loved in my youth. But from the age of 18 on I never lit up my third pack of the day without cursing him a little.

I finally went cold turkey, and have come to blame my years of smoking on my own weak will and bad character.

However, if anyone would want me to describe sainthood, I might have to consider Kenny the day I went to visit him while his brother was out playing road hockey.

It is all in the way you perceive how a child of three smokes a cigar.

—1986-91

Just Singing Along

We all sang Johnny Horton's "The Battle of New Orleans" as if we were not singing about a battle that celebrates our own defeat.

The song was banned in deference to the Queen visiting Canada, but was put back on again as soon as she left.

"The bloody British" we sing about chasing are ourselves. That is, regiments from Fredericton and Ottawa.

We all sing "Rainy Night in Georgia" and "Georgia on My Mind," though most of us have never seen a pecan tree.

But Georgia becomes the Maritimes for Maritimers when they are out west—"Those Old Cotton Fields Back Home" becomes the half-acre of potatoes your father planted in Bartibog.

Maritimers in Toronto can relate to the song about being stuck in Detroit City while dreaming of rural life.

We sing about every single city in United States, though few of use get to to there. We just adopt. Young men and women belting out "(Going back to) Houston" probably means they are heading home to Bathurst, New Brunswick, or Truro, Nova Scotia. It's even funnier if they are singing it with a French accent, and somehow more poignant.

A "rebel yell" is something Maritimers could always do. It seems to me that most Maritimers worth their salt sympathize with the south.

Don Williams sings about "Good Ole Boys Like Me," and for six months it was top on our charts—though he talked about cotton wool, Thomas Wolfe's novels, the Civil War, Tennessee Williams' plays, and Hank Williams' songs.

We've heard more stories about the Mexican Federalies than we've ever heard about our own police. Sing about white lightning and poisonous swamp snakes when we are at a community centre in January. I think, quite honestly, we've heard about the Vietnam war so much, in movie and song, that half of us think we're veterans.

Willie and Waylon are our outlaws as much as anyone's, and when Hank Jr. says, "The Mississippi River is runnin dry/ but a country boy can survive," all we have to do is think of the Miramichi.

Nor do I have much argument with this.

Hell, I love Hank Jr.'s daddy as much as anyone, and I know exactly what he means when he sings, "I'm So Lonesome I Could Cry," or whispers, "Men with Broken Hearts."

At least we're allowed to stand in a reflection from the light. We foster our patriotism from America's bankroll. There are friends of mine who love the song "The Ballad of the Green Berets" and those who hate it. Believing, for or against, that it is their song.

I know Canadians who sing Merle Haggards' "You're Walking on the Fighting Side of Me (running down our country, Lord)," as if they were ready to attack somebody by the throat.

There is no reason whatsoever we shouldn't have patriotism. If we can't get it from our own nation we'll get it where we can.

This should be perfectly obvious.

I've seen four movies about Eddie Rickenbacker, while in the one film Canada has made Billy Bishop was almost called a charlatan by his own countrymen.

The gap in the principle is so wide it's not worth discussion.

But as Yeats says, too long a sacrifice makes a stone of the heart. If we aren't allowed to love who we are, millions of us will adopt the love that singers give to another country.

For that's what all of these songs are saying and doing. They are sculptured verses of love of their country by ordinary men and women. Nothing much more than that.

And we love our own country so much that we've brought back their songs and adapted them, because we refuse to be speechless.

—1989

Our Magazines

When, a number of years ago, I first picked up one of the large magazines about the fishing industry, foolish me thought it would be about our fishing industry. Wrong. It was about United States'. We just buy it and read it in Canada. It's as if, by having this one, we don't need one of our own.

This was at the time when Newfoundland was still concerned about offshore over-fishing by foreign trawlers, and had petitioned the government in Ottawa a number of times for some support. Joe Clark was Minister of External Affairs at the time, so you know what kind of no-nonsense heavyweight they had in their corner.

But there was no article concerning this. Well, why should there be? And of course with only one cod fish left—Newfoundland has gotten over their concern. High time too.

Yet, one of the finest articles I ever scanned in this particular magazine was about how to "avoid detection and/or prosecution" while fishing in foreign waters. Of course, for this magazine, "foreign" means Canada—primarily on Georges Bank. In a way, it's kind of like complicity, supporting someone else's plan to break into your house.

I first saw this magazine in one of the shops in Saint John soon after I moved here in 1988, and have since seen it in Fredericton and Halifax.

When I was a kid, I used to buy hunting magazines, and fishing magazines. There are things I learned from them: How to convert Vietnam weaponry for backyard fun. How to dry plug for catfish. I've read about "Those Magnificent Bonefish," and "How to Stalk the Elusive Swamp Buck of Alabama."

I did get close: "Those Hidden Muley's" got me about 3,000 miles away—still slightly out of range of my old .303 British, even though my eyes are pretty good and I had put a scope on it.

They told me that to shoot my "Muley" I should first fly to O'Hare airport in Chicago and to be prepared for a hard go "up there in the wilds." But there are no direct flights from Saint John to O'Hare—so I had to travel through Boston. And there is not a Canadian yet who has not been stuck in Logan airport for a day or more. So I missed my connecting flight.

I came back reeling from the experience and relived it to my cousins.

"Knock Down Your Own Bear, With Only a Dog and a Pistol."

Well, here pistols aren't allowed, and I wouldn't hunt with a dog, and as a matter of fact, I don't see the great sport or need in killing a bear. But the point is, those who do hunt bears here seem, for the most part, to have a different attitude about the whole process.

"Now You Too Can Look Like a Tree."

I know it would be nice to look like a tree—and in the picture everything except the arrow tips are camouflaged on this lad whose body is as expressionless as a spruce root.

When you read these articles in these magazines you're always asked to go and buy something "available at your local hunting store," whether it's the US Department of the Navy's corrode-proof twine, or US Department of the Interior's water-resistant flares—these items never seem to get here in quantities we all need.

I try to keep up.

I've read about sleeping under silky webs to keep spiders at bay, noiseless $200 boots, and how to have fun with your muzzle-loaded squirrel gun. This article talked about finding a tree with eight squirrels, which, as good as it was, wasn't as good as the old days when you could find a tree with 16.

"Snakes are Bad—Falling 2,000 Feet is Worse."

Tells us what to do when chasing goats along a winding path in the Rockies, and how not to start a rock slide which would bury us up to our neck.

"Quiet Is as Quiet Does—Stalking the Montana Big One in Your Bare Feet."

"American Pride Means American Turkey."

or those who would

"Use a Pistol for the *Coup de Grâce*."

And there is always wild boar hunting at a private boar farm in California—"A Kill Is 100% Guaranteed. Just Ask For Willie."

If a Maritimer were to take one-quarter of the suggestions he finds in these magazines seriously, he'd be in the looney bin. But I swear, I've heard people making a case for the authenticity of sneaking about the New Brunswick bush in buckskins, trying to relive a mythology that isn't ours, with Davy Crockett hats on our heads.

If we wish to talk about illiteracy we are illiterate in this way. We are glutted with information that is either almost absolutely irrelevant to us, or makes us part of someone else's hinterland.

And the worst part of all of this is, Bass! You know it and so do I. I will make a bet that in the last 12 issues of any one of these outdoor magazines the word "Bass" will be found in an article title. Not the word "Salmon" or "Grilse" or "Fly-fishing"—but the words "Bass Fishing—Fun With Those Early Morning Big Mouths."

May they rot.

—1990

Lockhartville and Kevin O'Brien

Those who adapted Alden Nowlan's writings to the stage, in the play, *Lockhartville*, made the same mistake as those who directed Treat Williams and Ann-Margaret in Tennessee Williams'play, *A Streetcar Named Desire*.

These mistakes were improvisations to fit the times we now live in. Kind of like the Restoration poets fiddle-faddling with Shakespeare because Shakespeare was vulgar.

In *Streetcar*—the one I've seen, with Treat Williams and Ann-Margaret—they had to change the thrust of the play in order to do it.

Because, in today's fashionable concepts of relevant literature, only men should be held accountable for actions taken. Ann-Margaret was not allowed to be the Blanche Dubois that Tennessee Williams wrote about. That is, she was never complex enough to be finally tragic.

She was outwardly made stronger (of course) and given outwardly at least more intelligence (of course, again) and this allows the brilliance of Williams' Blanche Dubois to be lost. For the director was not courageous enough to show that it lay in her own self-delusion and self-sabotage. The lack of courage is in the fact that we must all pretend to believe, like certain feminists do, that Blanche should no longer be capable of self-deception.

Within this particular 1980s interpretation, Blanche never had to be forgiven her delusion and anger; and Stanley, as a man, couldn't be. So the play is allowed to fail.

What is extremely relevant to the play—Blanche Dubois' subtle but willing involvement in sexual intercourse—becomes in this interpretation, sexual abuse.

So instead of the tragedy of three lives, the play breaks apart. It becomes another tiresome, self-congratulatory chronicle of a woman's pain.

In this, there has been a narrowing of focus and a diminishing of sympathy for years. All in the name of progressive concern.

If a writer is good then he must be on our side. This is what I've learned, when I hear otherwise competent people talk a kind of readjustment to literature.

For instance, if Tolstoy was great, then *War and Peace* is an indictment against war rather than a novel about all humanity. Therefore, it made no difference to Tolstoy that the Russians won, or that bravery was shown on the field. (Ahem)

The work of Alden Nowlan, when adapted to the stage in *Lockhartville*, suffers the same fate as that of Williams and Tolstoy. For, in many ways, the same ground is covered.

So much of the literary criticism in our country is supplied by sophisticated illiterates. They have never been able to understand what it is they are reading.

I have written enough, and read enough balderdash about what I've written, to know this is absolutely true.

We can catalogue some of the do's and don't's of academic criticism almost without looking at a review:

If you work in the physical world then you must be poor.

No one loses his finger while working on his own automobile who is not unread.

Being unread is a rural phenomenon, and as such is bad.

If there is a rusted car up on blocks in a character's backyard, you can almost bet he's slept with his daughter, whether the writing indicates that or not.

Working men are written about to be exposed, never admired.

Many of my characters earn more money than the critics who simply assume that they are downtrodden. And think with greater clarity and ultimately more kindness besides.

The worst thing you can do today is to imply more than immediately meets the eye. Because today's literary ideas are reduced to accommodate a stereotype that often comes from our educated sense of privilege.

And this is what has followed Alden Nowlan to the stage.

Lockhartville is an adaption of Alden's work—not only of Kevin O'Brien but of his poetry and ideas from his stories. It has been around awhile playing on stages here and there.

Various Persons Named Kevin O'Brien is the story of a man remembering his childhood and adolescence, of growing up in real poverty in Nova Scotia in the '30s and during the war years. It is a good novel, better than good, sound in generous feeling, and I read it in galley form before it was published.

The last thing Alden Nowlan's writing has is the first thing the play wants to demonstrate: A visceral cynicism for the life of the father, Judd O'Brien, and indeed most of the men in the play, and an unquestioning belief that all Judd's motives are mean spirited, cowardly and brutal. This overshadows everything—the idea of rural life and the incorporated poem, "The Bull Moose"; the idea of the Canadian men at Ypres and the incorporated poem, "Ypres: 1915."

What is aggravating about this is not that it's just an interpretation, but an interpretation which seriously and perhaps humbly felt it had the source work's best intentions at heart. So it is difficult to be hard on something which never meant to ridicule.

But if this cynicism does not come from Nowlan's work, which I believe it never does, then it comes from outside the work. It comes from an idea that the work is an exposé of what we already know, or more to the point, what we all should think.

There is a good deal of telling us all what we should think in this play.

All of it is based on the surface tensions of Nowlan's work, but it is not based in any concrete way on the ultimate understanding of humanity that Alden Nowlan's genius gave us.

Judd O'Brien becomes the archetypal father—a mean-spirited bully who taunts his sensitive son and worse—for this is the real injustice as far as the play is concerned—has no "understanding" of women.

In the play, Kevin is "sensitive" because he is confrontational with the ideas and symbols of his father's manhood—the moose rack, the army souvenirs, the talk about war—how he hates it, and is sympathetic to the problems of his sister and his mother who need to escape a type of patriarchal hell.

Although the play, in one sense, is an indictment against patriarchy, Alden's own work was always far more subtle and encompassing.

Judd's actions in the play never come out of belittled dreams. His actions are never seen to be fumblingly tender as they are in *Various Persons Named Kevin O'Brien*.

The one thing you know from reading *Various Persons Named Kevin O'Brien* is that Alden Nowlan loved and sympathized with Judd O'Brien because he understood him and on more than one occasion at least partly agreed with him. He also shows us time and again how the man tries to be tender.

The last thing we're allowed to do in watching the play, *Lockhartville*, is agree with Judd O'Brien or think a man like him could be tender.

There is a sentiment struck like a gong that all his likes are male likes and therefore must be distrusted. Such as booze, hunting, misogyny, and gloating war stories.

Alden was no misogynist and he understood female characters as well as most women writers today—and better than many. But the male-female relationships in the play are painted with such a broad brush it becomes absurdly one-sided and therefore absolutely pejorative.

No one has repressed the idea of a woman's role in the world of the 1940s more then the standard ideologists of the 1980s. One only has to have known my two grandmothers to know this. One who had grade eight education and started her own theatre business—which allows some people to think I was born in great luxury—

the idea of money and what it's used for is another problem academics have never solved; and my maternal grandmother who held at bay, with a doubled-barrelled shotgun, creditors from a bank.

And like Tolstoy, it is Alden Nowlan's humanity that makes Alden Nowlan care about the men and women involved in war.

But none of the patriotic humanity found in "Ypres: 1915" was found in the play when "Ypres: 1915" was discussed, because the actors in the play were too busy trying to prove to the assembly that they were above honouring discussions about battles.

In fact, the very antithesis of why Alden Nowlan wrote the poem happens in the play to "Ypres: 1915." It is trivialized.

The same things that would disturb a peace activist from, oh, let's say—Charlottetown of 1986—disturb the Kevin O'Brien of Lockhartville of 1944.

That is instead of being a young man of the '30s and '40s, he is a traumatized quasi-feminist of the 1980s, filled with a trembling angst and caustic one-dimensional nature. He never, as Alden Nowlan's Kevin O'Brien does, speaks about nature or work or life as if he understands it. His father is the culprit, his sister is a victim, and he sides with his sister.

In the play, when Kevin fumbles with her panties it's because he sides with women, not because he'd like to sleep with one. You get the feeling that this Kevin O'Brien likes the feel of panties because the panties represent women's morally superior personalities.

So, too, there is in the play the overt testimony of incest between father and victimized daughter. It comes not from

Alden's work. It comes from the stereotype of what *writing* about an ignorant working man must want us to believe.

A father probably sleeps with his daughter if he hunts and spits and talks about Ypres. And wouldn't Alden have wanted it represented that way—just like us?

But it's not the incest which is bothersome, only what it indicates. It is deceitful only in that so much else about Judd O'Brien is falsified. What does it matter if, after you demean and ridicule a man's spirit, you attach a sin?

It is just one more way to prove that he does not have to be loved. But the point is, in the novel, every act is finally understood and forgiven. Though not all are excused Kevin forgives not only his father, but himself and his sister as well. Far better than any young man or woman in Sociology 2000 would.

And, you see, that's the problem. In the play, art has become social work. Nothing more than a holding forth on a morally superior lifestyle. Much of it contrary to the novel's genius. A genius few of the players were compassionate enough to understand.

One of my problems with watching it was how many people from the university here seemed to like it. You got the feeling Dostoevsky once had: "If they are our teachers, what hope is there for us."

—1987

Lee Could Not Have Spoken

The grand old man of the Confederacy, General Lee's last words were spoken in delirium in 1870: "Tell Hill he must come up," and "Strike the tent."

The first, an order to A. P. Hill, the red flannel-wearing General who had saved Lee's Army of Northern Virginia in 1862. The second was spoken to an unknown orderly to take his tent down.

But now, after 120 years, they are being disputed. A College of Physicians insists that the damage Lee suffered in his stroke in the autumn of 1870 would not have permitted him to utter those words.

The trouble is the pedants are always right.

I have learned, however, that every time they stand on a point they usually want to diminish someone else's reputation, sometimes their entire lives. They never say this is their intent, but it is always evident in what they try to correct.

Lee could not have spoken.

In the fall of 1970, studying American History, I was told by an American professor that the Alamo had no heroes.

He hated the idea of war, and I can truly say I understand this. But because he did, he begrudged the very idea of heroics in war.

"There wasn't a hero there," he said to me. "They tried to surrender to Gen. Santa Anna when the fort capitulated, before Gen. Houston's troops arrived."

He seemed more than pleased with himself because of this opinion. One might ask, if he didn't believe in heroes, why was he so gleeful about what he obviously wanted me to consider a cowardly act?

At a party one evening in Fredericton, someone quoted a beautifully succinct line from one of C.S. Lewis' essays on Christianity.

"How can you believe him?" someone said. "He was a cocaine addict." This one phrase made him seem all-knowing, and C.S. Lewis a foolish old man indeed.

Another time, someone got angry and self-righteous because they heard Van Gogh had only cut his earlobe off, and didn't lop off the whole ear. It seemed that this action was not worth Van Gogh's entire life's work. And when he found out that Churchill had decided that Coventry should not be warned it was going to be bombed, so the Germans would not find out that the Brits had deciphered Germany's code, he said that Churchill was "no better than Hitler." And felt appalled. Which is what he said:

"I feel appalled."

The trouble is most of the rest of us tried to apologize to him. We were sorry Churchill did this, and could he forgive us.

"No—I'm just appalled."

There are always ways in which being stingily correct will reduce everyone else to our level.

We must get a great deal of pleasure out of it.

A woman I know sat in a poet's den one day and picked out the three or four spelling mistakes in his book of verse. She said nothing else about the book.

Of course it reduced everything to where she sat. She was only being helpful. Not capable of writing a book of verse herself, she was genuinely interested in only what was wrong with them.

"Oh—here's a mistake," were her first words after she had picked up the book.

"How right you are," the poet said, looking at it.

And she smiled around at us all.

The poet smiled too.

When I knew this woman, she continually used the method of convenient empathy. Faint praise not to damn, but to democratise. This is the same lady who every time you told her of someone being up for an award said, almost in tears: "Oh, I'm so afraid they'll lose." Until you realized that she was praying, that no one ever won anything—but herself.

These peculiar people come in all shapes and sizes, all races and religious affiliations. Their thoughts are programmed by CBC Radio talk, Oprah Winfrey, or MTV.

You meet them at any party you go to, all summer barbecues, and any skating rink too, and it is reputation they are after. They are the educated, unthinking, literal-minded. They always hold others accountable for the ability to think for themselves.

Even in this essay, to say that you admire General Lee is, for some of them, to be in favour of antebellum era slavery. You will be accused of racism for saying that the rebels fought well, with little to fight with.

(That is like saying that Churchill who admired Rommel was in favour of Hitler, or that thousands of troops, and generals who fought against Lee and affectionately called him Uncle Bobby were on his side. In fact, the first thing soldiers of the Army of the Potomac

45 ⬠

would say about a new commander was: "He might be good but he ain't yet fought Bobby Lee.")

You never win. As Tolstoy comments, the stupid always have the initial argument. Yet somehow God gives us grace. The pedants always fail. That's the thing. Wait long enough.

Those who ridiculed F. Scott Fitzgerald in those lonely '30s killed him, but never destroyed him, and don't matter a damn now. Or Dostoevsky, him.

Or General Grant's friends, who called him a drunk behind his back and went whining to Lincoln about him, never mattered much once Richmond fell.

But of course, beware. These people just change tack and keep going.

Not only do some of them change horses in midstream. They put on a different bridle and bit, and change the stream itself.

Some of them change opinions about people with the same grace as changing underwear.

"He couldn't have done that," or "She's not as good as you think," is forever on their lips, as a way to explain you to me, and to shore themselves up for tomorrow.

They never meet you on even ground, these ladies and gentlemen. They are forever at your throat, or at your feet. They are on every passion window in every church. But it is never themselves being nailed to the cross.

—1990

Stag Films, Teen Movies

Give credit where its due. Most porno films have something democratic about them. Most of them have an underlining contempt for the human body, male or female, and a cynicism for human emotion. Nor do they ever hide that fact. Contempt is almost always universal. Everyone is damned, and everyone knows it.

This can't be said for the dozens of goofy movies that millions of Canadian teenagers saw, from the late seventies to the late-80s.

In these movies there is very little democracy.

The basis for movies like *Porky's* (which explores the romantic exploits of a group of wacky grinning college teens, and which became the prototype for a dozen or more spin-off movies over the decade) is the idea that sex is liberating, and sexual liberty belongs to the young.

Belongs to those who are irreverent; especially to those who hate learning. (Try to study and someone is always throwing a chalk eraser at your head.)

And, to those who know that sex is—well certainly not sexual—but funny.

And that, what is funny must be healthy. So, therefore, get with it—it must be okay to do.

Yet no one in these movies is ever really irreverent, really spontaneous, or really funny.

These movies are kind of like the newly divorced dad at the party who laughs too loud and stands on his head too long, with a glass of beer on his feet, to pretend he is free at last. Free at last. Somehow it just don't work.

Well, these movies don't work, something like that. They deliberately overdo their hand, and then ask us to believe they're the real thing.

It's reasonable to say that for these movies to feel spontaneous they would first have to give more credit to the young, which they constantly pretend to glorify.

In these various teen movies, starting with *Porky's* and going through a number of others, there is a litany of what is thought to be acceptable and unacceptable to the youth in North America, who are supposedly privileged enough not to have to expect too much of themselves.

In these movies ugliness is always belittled, and so is obesity. So is thinness. And so is weakness. And shortsightedness. And age. And so is genuine talent.

And so are, not surprisingly, the sex organs of men and women.

That is, what never matters in porno films becomes fodder for jokes in the dozens of teen movies of the '80s.

All the stereotypes are true, and therefore supposedly uproarious and raucous.

The repressed teacher is really a sex kitten, and everyone knows that. Just as soon as she puts away the books and lets down her hair.

There is something immoral in the university president's background too, and we will find it out.

Because the real message, quite unknown to the cast themselves, is that everything is taboo.

The girls are really being naughty, the boys are doing something wrong—and that's what makes it all so funny.

No one can have sex if they understand chemistry, mathematics, or don't find jokes about big tits constantly amusing. And somehow only the young know this.

The old are too prudish, too respectable.

Yet the respectable turn out to be fakes. Because we find out, sooner or later, that they partake in the sex act also. And the message really is that the sex act is wrong.

We know the sex act is wrong because everyone is always "caught" while doing it.

There is a continual peeping and giggling and looking through crackholes, and climbing up ladders to look into dorm windows where the movie's pretty women disrobe in front of you.

Other women—such as the obese and ugly, always are seen doing something as ordinary as going to bed in pyjamas with their hair in curlers. Which is always looked upon as remarkably funny. Supposedly there should be no sexual feeling in certain bodies. And if there is it is always looked upon as hilariously perverse.

The first thing an average porno film understands is that the last thing sex is, is funny. And everyone gets equal time.

We can talk about another kind of teen movie: slasher films, like *Friday the 13th*. They work on the same theory of the non-allowability of the sexual act. And of the fear of genuine emotion.

Yet slasher movies don't even care to pretend sex is innocent. They start right out of the gate, condemning it with an axe to the forehead.

Though murder is nasty, those who are killed always deserve to die. In these films, sex kittens aren't repressed, they get slain for having a skimpy bra in their wardrobe.

Sex always carries a death sentence in a morbid, somehow sexual, way.

And a chase around a table almost always prolongs it.

The characters are usually caught at a camp or in a beach house with the power out. Jason, the perennial maniac in a hockey mask, waits until they are jumping into the sack with each other.

Or he pops up out of the water, kind of like one of our furry little Greenpeace-protected seals, with a hatchet.

Killing the sex kitten naked on a raft somehow suggests that she's engaged in something immoral. In these movies they actually do staple your forehead to the floor.

The murderer is wrong to kill, of course. But the real truth is the movie is set-up so everyone will cheer for the slasher.

Here the slasher does the peeping and the climbing of ladders to see the women disrobe.

And since the sex in these movies isn't funny the slasher will have to inform us that sex is still a despicable act—by killing almost everyone who partakes in it.

The script won't allow us to laugh at the obese or handicapped. It allows us to cheer while they are done in.

The fat woman has to climb a burning rope with a hot cross bun in her mouth.

And so it goes.

Almost everyone in these teen movies is not liked, and not likeable. There are always confrontations between the various victims before they are slain. Rude practical jokes, noises and childish interferences that supposedly pass for American teenage fun disrupt our sensibilities at every turn. You just don't give a man a chair: you place tacks on it first.

Never too bright, and hostile to authority figures, they drive in vans and talk about stereo equipment, believe in peace and are somewhat ecology-minded.

The actors of these teen comedies and slashers are interchangeable and the lessons they teach the same.

No porno film ever showed such little faith in humanity.

—1989

Caligula, Legere, and the Nature of Power

You're walking home—from a tavern—a bit drunk. You're singing a song you learned when you were in the navy ten years before, making up some of the words as you go.

It is a winter night—all the streetlights are out. You don't have much money. But what you have you've promised to bring home to your wife.

Just as you approach your street, you see someone standing alone off in the dark. He jumps you, and tries to steal your last few cents. You fight back. But suddenly you discover who it is.

You're so stunned that you let go of him and he runs off down the alley clutching your money in his hand, his toga flying, his spindly legs in their strapped leather thongs and his balding head visible under the cold light of the moon. He makes a dash around the corner and is gone.

The year is 39 A.D., under the consulship of the young Emperor Gaius Caesar (Caligula)—and you've just found out the hard way that the lad is bonkers. Is so much of a loon that he hangs about Rome at night to mug his own citizens. Some say it's for kicks, because he has nothing much else to do—others say it's because he loves the smell of money. (What's wrong with that?)

But what's worse is that you have to go home and explain this to your wife, who's been waiting to buy some bread and salt. Who in their right mind would believe a story like this?

Gaius believed he was a god—he also believed he was the son of a god and, as Suetonius tells us, he had his palace extended to the temple. Had the heads removed from various statues of the various gods, and had replicas of his own head put on. He became, in a way, all gods.

He would walk around and pray to himself, or ask himself favours.

"Rise me to heaven, or I'll send you to hell," he is reported to have told one god.

Others as well believed that Caligula was a god. He could, in fact, do anything he wanted. So perhaps it's far-fetched to think of an actual emperor, who could do anything he wanted, coming out of the darkness to mug you. (Imagine the likes of Bill Clinton doing such a thing.)

Gaius' ascension to the throne after the reign of Tiberius—a man so strong he could put his thumb through a boy's skull if he wanted, and sometimes he wanted—was viewed as "a real dream come true."

Except people found out they couldn't mention goats in front of him. No goats. Because by his mid-20s his head was balding, and he felt the mere mention of a goat was mockery against him. So he'd have your tongue taken out.

You had to crouch down when you passed him, somewhat like Groucho Marx did, because he couldn't stand anyone taller then he was, looking down at his bald spot. So people would, on pain of death, lower themselves about a foot when they went by:

"Bear in mind I can treat anyone exactly as I please."

For some reason that rarely meant opening the granary.

He was said to have sawn a group of theatre goers in half for not proclaiming him an immense genius, after his first stage production. (I see no difficulty here.)

The one thing of course, is that horror is somehow always funny in hindsight. I have known people to have laughed themselves silly over disembowelment. (However not their own.) Perhaps it keeps us sane.

And Suetonius makes no great distinction between being chopped up or disembowelled, or merely having your throat slit for sneezing, at a party in your own honour, as certain little boys had.

"I sworry I snweezed."

"Suffer the little children to come unto me," was not a big line with Gaius. It is an exceptional idea that Gaius was alive, not much more than a child, when these lines were first offered.

Also it is an exceptional idea, perhaps not consciously intended by Suetonius, that all evil is the same, and hatches the same crime. That the acts are different in different places, but that in fact there is only one evil perpetrated against the world, constantly and always, and forever the same. That they are continually linking together like a giant D.N.A. to form the one monstrous complexity of deceit.

All crimes essentially are formed within the same framework, and have one body. And all those who suffer from the pieties of power and empowerment, are suffering from the same crime.

Those who suffered under Caligula are the same as those who suffered by the hands of Allan Legere.

Legere sniggering as he washed the Downey sisters' blood from his body is the same sniggering Caligula afforded his entourage. It cannot possibly be different.

Suetonius talks about Caligula mocking Claudius, as well as having an old man dress up as a gladiator to face an equally decrepit lion (as you can imagine, people were rolling in the aisles over this one), to cutting the tongues out of knights, and having children slaughtered.

As he tells it, it all seems to be the same sin.

Now, whether Gaius was mad because he drank out of one too many lead goblets, who's to say. There was more than enough lead goblets to go around, and not everyone proclaimed his horse a senator. "Let them hate me as long as they fear me," he often said.

"If I were you, I'd fear ME," I remember Legere telling a boy at the pool hall one summer day in 1966.

Gaius made the court philosopher Seneca the brunt of his mania often enough. Until Seneca wisely noted:

"No one can instill fear, except in the amount they have in themselves." This is appropriate not only for an emperor but for the small-time hood as well. It is not one iota different.

Gaius must have had some fairly lonely nights, when he was not stealing his friends' brides at their weddings, or hopping in bed with his sisters.

He must have realized on those brief excursions into the dark, as he saw his reflection in the ditchwater, that madness isn't entirely the fault of ones stars.

And finally, like Legere, he must have understood that he only thought he was in control.

"I can do anything I please," must have on occasion sounded hollow to him. For it must naturally be followed by: "What else can I do?"

(Funny enough, these are very comparable to the lines Legere is reported to have uttered at his capture: "I could have done this—I could have done that. My name is Allan Legere.")

Neither could ever seem to do enough. Both were self-agitated by inner loathing. Eventually, Caligula was murdered in his garden. His wife and children were murdered shortly after that.

Although Suetonius calls Christianity a "mischievous sect," and categorizes Gaius' persecution of the Christians as one of his good acts, there is some comparable reasoning with it.

Suetonius, like Saint Paul, is too observant not to see the toadyism of high culture and false humanity, the rancid perfume that covers up the vomit of vanity.

Suetonius tries to let us understand these men in physical terms, because he wants to warn us "that their bodies are their limitation when compared to some greater ideal." And this is what we come to realize again and again throughout history. That the torture chamber and the knifing on a side street shows that power always leaves the greatest ideal out.

Suetonius' fault lies in his problem of not really knowing what this greater ideal is. He knows there is one—he knows the Emperors should have it. He is unsure as to why they do not hold it.

He does not know that the very thing they have limits their ability. Power eclipses the one idea that surmounts it—humility.

Yet he allows us to understand, in his great 2000-year-old book, that the power of Gaius is not much more than the power of Legere when looking down from the stars. And hell walks in little Italy wearing a $2000 suit.

The inescapable dilemma of all men and women is that they need to use whatever power they have to prove again and again to themselves, that it is theirs.

—1993

Power Games

The human response to power is to become enmeshed in it. And power is considered a good thing to seek. Why is it considered good, and even moral? Because those who seek power now are self-deluded into thinking that they have never sought it before.

We know this is what the neo-Nazis seek. They recently had cross burnings in Alberta and Washington state. One talked of his shotgun as being a womb renovator—an instant birth control method.

Anyone who speaks like this is banal. At its most reduced denominator, power always is.

Five years ago, in New Orleans, at a party in the French Quarter, a very respectable well-to-do man from the university said the same thing. Except he was considered and probably still is considered a humanist, a progressive thinker. He never spoke of hurting anyone. He never spoke of shotguns. He spoke against shotguns. He spoke against those who have shotguns. He spoke in an impassioned way for a social betterment program that would convince the people he disliked to become more like him. To change their "value system," their "birth control methods," and the importance they put upon today's "religious structure." Whatever else it sounded, it sounded wise. He did not want to remove his opposition from the face of the earth like the neo-Nazi cross burner in Alberta did, he wanted to enlighten their thoughts to become like his.

As a matter of fact, all the people in the world who would dare disagree with him were called Nazis.

But after his talk, no longer could we ever think of the progressive-minded saying: "Live and let live." To be progressive, to be a Nazi, is not to be able to leave others alone.

The Church of Jesus Christ, Christian-Aryan Nations would never say "Live and let live," either. In their constant diatribes that appeal to the hinterland of the white mind they snigger at Jews, Catholics, Indians and Blacks. Truthfully it is painful to listen to them, because they have abandoned themselves to the psychotic emblems of tyranny.

The progressive who spoke in New Orleans, with a few select *bon mots* to make us laugh—because he wanted to show that he was human also and could tell a good joke—disliked the Catholics immensely (of course he had friends who were Catholics and whom agreed with him) and wished to, in a way, indoctrinate the rest. He spoke in a way, like those in the Aryan Nations spoke, except he was going to educate and enlighten, and raise the consciousness of others. He didn't want to kill them...yet.

But, if their world is going to change, it has to change according to *his* agenda.

And this is what we see so much behind the eyes of the argument, a venal grasping toward the darkness of our point of view.

These are considered saintly values by both poles. I mean both of these philosophies are formulated from the coarse hemp of what is truly holy.

The Aryan Assembly of God believes that they are doing God's work. They consider themselves the disciples of a new order, and they readily display their devotion to God and Country. They rarely acknowledge *The Bible* they quote from as being written by the Jews. And of course they stand on the very free speech they would destroy in others.

The progressives are ever mindful of their significance in the universe, their destiny to change things for the better. And if they have to eradicate works of literature—or what is considered the bogeyman by some of them—the male canon of literature—in order to do it, they will. Listen long enough and you will realize that free speech is finally on the table with them as well.

The neo-Nazis may watch Rambo in *First Blood* and understand God and Country. The progressives watch, oh, for argument, *The Last Temptation of Christ*.

Rambo, the action hero, is significant to the neo-Nazies because it shows the infallibility of their point of view.

The Last Temptation of Christ is significant to the progressives because it shows Christ to be fallible like they are. As one woman promoting the movie said: "After seeing this—I now can agree with him."

Because, you see, in her interpretation, Christ was not so much filled with radical love, as he was a radical. And this is what the progressives that have boasted so much about change feel they themselves are.

If you are on one side, an Aryan, or on the other, a progressive, you can sooner or later excuse your humanity.

Take all life, take Christ himself, for what you want and not perhaps for what it, or he, is.

Whatever they agree with it is sometimes difficult to see how Christ, or even common sense, could agree with them.

I am certain that power, whether it is in the Feminist movement, in the Black movement, in the Irish Republican Army, in PEN International, or in the "Aryan Nations," destroys us. Yet, it is what almost all of us seek, almost all of the time.

—1991

Quebec: Je me souviens

When I was in Virginia, an English-studies professor told me that in student dorms, in the mid-'70s, the picture that went along side the martyred revolutionary, Che Guevara, was Quebec's premier, René Lévesque.

She thought that not only would I understand this, but I would, like herself, rejoice in it. That, as a liberal thinker, (and what other kind is there?) I would see Quebec's struggle in terms of oppressed and oppressor. That the only vision of Canada I should have was the vision of Canada that she, as an American, had. That is, a Canada with an English majority stomping its boot on the throat of a French minority.

"They only want freedom, don't they?" she said to me.

When I told her that Quebec might separate she said without missing a beat:

"Oh, I hope they do," in the same tone she would have used when talking about abused housewives leaving their husbands.

And that's the point. The separatist voices of Quebec have fought to establish this rather one-dimensional perception about their "struggle." How wonderful it is to be sad and oppressed when you teach economics at the university.

What the doctor, Che Guevara, and the journalist, René Lévesque, had in common was that both of them at a certain time were able to tap into the font of sympathy-for-the-victim in the American physic.

Make no mistake it is sympathy, which sooner or later will run you over.

The woman from Virginia knew very little about Canada. But ignorance carries moral presumption; so the plight of my nation was reduced to what happened in Longfellow's *Evangeline*, and she hoped, for the sake of "the gallant people of Quebec," that this was still not happening.

Then, not waiting for a reply, she looked away from this English Canadian, blinked back tears and acted the rest of the evening as if I had displeased her.

Don't get me wrong. My argument is not with her. It's further north. Because most of our intellectuals have postured in the same self-congratulatory way for the last 25 years.

The woman was not much different than us. She had absolutes when thinking about power and victimization.

Such absolutes about power and victimization have become the only way to think for enlightened people.

It was as popularly uncivilized, when I was Writer-in-Residence at the Uunversity of New Brunswick in the '80s, amongst the educated circles I knew at that time, to think that English Canada might have a case, inside or outside of Quebec, as it was to think that white supremists had a case.

Let's face it, in universities, if you questioned Quebec, 80% of the intellectuals thought you were a part of the lunatic fringe. They would look at each other with rather bemuffled frowns and astonished eyes.

At any rate, past all the 6s and 7s, this has left the vast majority of Canadians outside the province of Quebec isolated from any interpretation of their country.

People, millions of them, who do not teach at university, or pontificate on *Morningside*, or work for the media.

And so, most of them have long ago stopped interpretating it, insisting on one thing only, that if Quebec goes, the last thing they are going to do is shake their hand and mince pleasantries with them at the door.

I think that's bloody fair overall. Yet, even this, this one last act of defiance against the power brokers who have at times pissed in their faces, is held against them.

"How dare we be unconcerned. Now more then ever we need to show a conciliatory side to Quebec," a friend from Ottawa said recently. "And," he continued, "we all know who the destroyers of Canada are—REFORM."

No matter what I think of Reform, and to tell the truth it is not a great deal, it didn't seem to register to him, that Lucien Bouchard sits across the floor, and an adroit political reptile, Parizeau, heads the Parti Québécois. But there is a kind of moral cowardice inherent in the Canadian position. The established idea is to always show moderation in principle, rather than in temperament. That is Thomas Payne's statement about where virtue and vice lie, in reverse.

I've had to listen to an American intellectual in Amherst, Massachusetts, tell a woman from Laval, in a room filled with Canadian Embassy officials, who were throwing a party for him, paying the bill, that he at least was sorry that there was no representative from "her country" present. And no one thought that this was insensitive or inappropriate. Or downright stupid.

Except for the woman, herself, who, blushing, said that her representatives were already there and she was happy they were.

"Of course," he said, taking a hurried angst-filled sip of his expensive wine, "but you and I know what I mean."

Then he looked about and everyone decided it diplomatic to change the subject. Which is fine. But you got the feeling that he thought he was saying what was appropriate—was surprised he wasn't. I think this was the greater part of the insult, that he simply assumed that "right thinking" people like ourselves could forgo nationalism and smirk and jibe about the breakup of our country—a place he had yet to go.

And, as he spoke in his polished Southern way I was reminded, as I am with so many learned people I've met who shout the loudest for freedoms, that there are many amongst them, who just a generation ago, would have told "frog" jokes at parties, played Jim Crow and kept the "nigger" down.

But I suppose the worst thing in all of this—more unforgivable than cowardice itself, is to be a constant apologist for who you are. By being an apologist while fearing the truth is even worse.

But the truth will wait. The questions Quebec will finally have to answer for herself will wait.

Much of the problem, through Meech and Charlottetown, was that understandable human emotions and concerns of countrymen were almost always looked upon incredulously by people from Ottawa. Since emotion was in bad taste, let's broker a deal through economics.

However, these same people made allowances for Quebec emotion when these deals failed. Tramping Quebec's *Fleur-de-lis* was unforgivable, but Quebec boys ripping the Canadian flag was so understandable that it was naively and childishly shown on CBC time and again as proof of dire warnings coming true.

Confederation has so often been a matter of convenience for Ontario and Quebec, with the rest of us as appendages of some kind, that until ten years ago no one else was considered terribly important in the country. Nor, therefore, did the country really matter in any cognitive way to those who held most of the power cards. Nor did they know it or understand it as a whole. Still this idea of Canada, as a whole, is on an entirely shaky foundation. Big brothers rarely come to little sisters defence here. In the eternal scheme of things they are more likely to rat on you to the neighbours.

In reality, my thought is this: Newfoundland has more to fear from Canadian policy then Quebec ever had.

And was betrayed more. Lucien Bouchard was ambassador to France during that time the French were threatening us with warships to protect "their fishery" from Newfoundland.

There is a curious parallel here—between Newfoundland's needs and Quebec's importance. Bouchard, absolutely provincial-minded, with no idea of what Canada was, came home frightened, and hoped someday to prove that he was not a Canadian. (He is doing a good job).

Mulroney, of course, not knowing that leading a country might mean you needed moral courage to stand your ground, went to arbitration. In the end Newfoundland was left to hang and dry. The cod are gone and the seals prosper on the squid jiggin' grounds.

But reasons of mismanaged federal-provincial affairs are not why Quebecers will go.

It's precisely the opposite reason. All of this tedious compromise shows Canadians to be the people Americans laugh at and Quebecers love to hate. Where compromise works it will never endear. Never at all.

Quebec looks good in this age of fractional re-zoning. So perhaps there is nothing wrong with their rezoning also.

But the fault, finally, will not be with Canadian chauvinism. Nothing that is Canadian has ever handcuffed Quebec's identity, any more than Quebec's identity has limited Canadian action in its national and international affairs.

We are being blindsided by our own left hook. And staggering about lamely to throw it again.

In reality, we're both colonies on the far-flung baggage train of the United States. Which, if Quebec goes it alone, she will learn soon enough.

Quebec nationalists, like Lucien Bouchard, have only contempt for the country in which Parliament they are a part of.

Be it as it may, in 1861, when Mississippi decided to succeed from the Union, Jefferson Davies, with all the manners of a Southern gentleman, went home. He did not continue to sit in that country's Senate to collect a pension.

This is something that my friend from Virginia would never have understood about Quebec's privileged position in Canada, nor, I imagine, have taken the time to be corrected upon.

Where falsehoods are convenient they are most often ingrained.

—1992

Bed and Breakfasts

The worst thing I find about life in the Maritimes is not the poverty—hell, my apologies to all those who think that it is moose hunting—or even the fixed link from Prince Edward Island—no, it is not even that—it is Bed and Breakfasts. And my deep apologies, also, to those who like them or own them.

Nothing more artificial or more touted as genuine has ever existed—except perhaps some novella by an academic writer.

Imagine going across town to spend a night in a stranger's house? Or worse still, a stranger's house with rules? That is about the best sense of comfort you can have at these places.

It seems to me that the whole point of Bed and Breakfasts is that right away we must be pleased that we are being deprived. And that part of the "sophisticated romance" is to pay for it.

That this is how people once lived—or (since B&B's are always polemical in my view) this is how we should be living.

The telephone is two flights down, and you can't use it after 10 PM anyway because the "parlour" is locked. If there is a television, try not feeling guilty and unsophisticated if you ask for it.

Its usually tucked away in another room—simpler in concept than the parlour, and similar in tone to the detox I was once in when I was trying to come off booze.

There are only two channels to watch anyway—and if the CANADA CUP is on one, and a three hour long special about a beekeeping festival somewhere in Quebec is on the other—there would be no winning the argument over what we would watch.

Smoking is almost always fanatically frowned upon: recently in Newfoundland, I could only smoke standing up, with my head out the window. But you are supposed to understand why this is of course; realize that it is you who are at fault—and do it for the good of the group.

That's the best thing about these places—a sense of communal blame can be attached to you as soon as you walk in. That is the way the fraternity-minded have always been.

You are given two keys when you enter, and sometimes three. I was once given four keys and a friend of mine swears she was given five. Two for the outside door alone. Its great to know that the first thing they do at the place you are about to stay is lock you out. One key was for my bedroom, and one for the communal toilet down the hall. The lady said she was given an extra one for the closet where tampons and a shower cap, were kept.

This is absolutely true. I wouldn't make this up. It is too horrible. It is far worse then the dt's I was in in the spring of 1982 after a three month drunk. I swear to God, when Trapper came in to cart me off to the hospital I was in finer fiddle then I was during a snowy weekend at a Bed and Breakfast.

Nothing prepares you for the kind of forced civility you meet from the owners at bedtime or breakfast. It is by and large the same type of uncontested civility found at craft fairs.

You always have the suspicion, that this great authenticity has been imported by failed Brits or Americans over the last 25 years. Just like so much of the theories about what the Maritimes must be, have been.

The magazines found in the bedrooms are the kinds of Atlantic magazines that no one in the Maritimes reads. This is because the owners themselves read them, or want to let on they do, and we are all supposedly like-minded.

B&B's will never have a broad cliental from actual Maritimers themselves, but they don't want it. In fact, their rules and lifestyles are there so they can rebuke them. For the most part it is an idea of what passes for Maritimes genuinity they wish preserved. And they will have it preserved. For those who do inhabit these places certainly must believe in them. And, as has been said, something not alive won't roll over and die.

In a way, too, it is like visiting an historical settlement in Bartibog. These houses were once owned by your grandparents and there is nothing startling in them, except how the new owners seem to miss the whole point of life.

—1991

Hunting

A man said to me, recently, at a dinner in Toronto, when it was mentioned that I had hunted moose, that he thought it quite appalling. That it might be alright if the "aboriginal nations" hunted and fished—but that white men should never again be allowed to. Then he smiled at me, with the mocking intent of pleasant men who feel suddenly that they now hold the irreproachable view. (It was the view of the rest of the table. I was the odd man out.)

These were all men and women preparing to leave Toronto the next morning to travel to an Indian reserve, to do some general sightseeing, and to get to know "a way of life." None had been to an Indian reserve before—and what struck me as preposterous was that they looked upon this the way some look upon going to a craft fair.

This is how the conversation evolved: The man who spoke to me was a Canadian from Kingston, Ontario, but there were other nationalities at the table who readily agreed with him—a woman from India, a man from Britain. Some people were eating fish, some beef.

At any rate, he wasn't preaching a new religion, this fellow from Upper Canada. It is the standard thought now in large and small urban centres—or you can bet he wouldn't have held it.

In most cities I've been to, if you say you know men who trap beaver, most people will expect you to say how odious you think these men are.

If you refuse to say this, you can bet less conversation will be directed toward you, and more conversation will be directed at you.

It's almost as if they've seen you go out an boot a seal in the head.

Sitting there, I was again reminded, that there are great safe targets in our world, some of which aren't animals. In fact, half my friends have become them—and sometimes their entire lives are trivialized in the process.

To know some of the men and women I have had the fortune to know, and then to listen to their lives being explained away by those who would never want to know them is something of a balancing act between two worlds. It's like listening to a woman who takes day trips up to the Miramichi to write about it, being called wise. It never quite fits, and never matters that it doesn't.

That, in some ways, is the problem I've noticed with notional knowledge as opposed to actual experience. The general ignorance of notional knowledge has always carried moral presumptions actual experience does not need to.

An animal rights activist from London, England, on television a few years ago felt an international committee of environmentalists should decide in what direction Canadians should accommodate the natural resources of their country. Because we ourselves were too backward to do it.

He too made "allowances" for the aboriginals. You got the feeling that he knew absolutely nothing about Canada, and had never been here. Never picked pine cones, or blueberries. *Never* saw a clear cut, *or* watched a water bomber, except in a picture.

But this is never considered problematic. For Canada, to both Americans and Brits, is still a colony.

Nor is it ever considered that each square block of his large city has removed and slaughtered 10,000 animals.

And it is, of course, a patronizing idea that the aboriginals "know" and the white men "don't know." I mean, patronizing toward the native Indian.

There is nothing more slighting than to give undo credit to some group for a certain prowess, when you secretly believe the quality that determines such a prowess depends on an "uncivilized" trait you yourself would be loathe to possess.

But hunters, whether white or Indian, man or woman, come in all sorts. I've hunted with all. Some are wonderful human beings, and others are not. Some of them know, and others do not. It does not matter to me what is thought of hunting (even seal hunting) in certain sections of Bromley, England, during the off-season.

Indians, as well as whites, do not hunt. Indians, as well as whites, will only hunt on occasion.

Indians, as well as whites, will slaughter and cripple and trap moose out of season, will chase animals down on snowmobiles, and will look upon them as commodities for the black market.

Some will say the Indians are only expressing a valid political point.

Fine enough for the point. Not so great for the moose.

At any rate, I know men who have no regard for animals. Or at least believe it is a terrible weakness to show regard.

I know others who have hunted and hardly killed. Have had the gun raised, and could not bring themselves to fire.

And still a third group, who have hunted, have killed, and still have a tremendous respect for the life around them.

These men and women are not incompatible with each other. As a matter of fact, I have friends from all these groups.

The real truth is, these groups are fluid and there is never an easy demarcation line. One sentiment often joins another in a single man or woman.

And until we are all vegetarians by our own choice, I will sympathize with the best of them. And I will try to make a point of distinguishing between the best and the worst.

Chekhov once said, regarding an aged Tolstoy, that he believed steam engines and electricity showed as much love of humanity as chastity and vegetarianism. It is a sentiment I find hard to disagree with.

If hunting is not misused by those who wish to eliminate it as an activity (and it is often misunderstood), it is often misrepresented to suit certain aims.

This was true at the University of New Brunswick, where I was in the '80s.

The department I was in was mainly made up of Americans and Brits, who had consciously insulated themselves from the rest of New Brunswick. Hunting was never a fashionable activity with them. I was openly questioned about it on many occasions, at times ungraciously, at times smugly. So smugly, it fact, that I took up hunting again.

But in a way, most New Brunswick life was misunderstood, to a certain extent, by them. Almost nothing of New Brunswick, except for day-trips into the country, was known to some of them.

And I remember the Soviet Olympic team marching into Calgary in 1988, all wearing fur coats and hats (which looked exceptionally Russian) and proud of being so dressed. They received not a whisper of protest by those angst-filled boys and girls in Vancouver who had threatened to disrupt the Olympics because of a timber wolf cull in Canada.

Their reasoning, at the time, might have been that such a working class state could not afford anything but sable.

The anti-hunting activists I've talked to (and I've talked to a few) make this mistake: They believe that no one has thought before what they now think. That what is needed is a raising of consciousness. That no hunter understands his soul as they do theirs. That, in fact, their souls are better. They leave out 1000 years of literature about the moral conflict in a person's soul over killing animals written by those who have killed.

It is, in all its fury, a fundamentalist perception fostered through limited contact with that which they hate.

I think it's fair to say, also, that people from London, England—the kind that mailed letter bombs to a friend of mine who worked at Canada House during the height of the seal hunt debates—have a very limited and slanted opinion of the sanctity of life.

And there was as much power play as piety in their policy seeking. But activism swells the breast of people.

There is a good deal of post-Christian saviourism in any number of them.

The New Testament has been replaced by the shuffle in the courtroom where we can get things done.

During the seal hunt debates, actresses would fly in from Los Angeles, get their picture taken with a seal, and pay a fine in court, while the media followed them back to their limo.

And three-quarters of those acquaintances of mine who are now activists for some cause—or, in a way, all causes—were artists of some sort in 1974. Whether blowing glass or taking photos.

They are not now artists, but have taken it upon themselves to tell others how they should live.

Their road veered off in the direction of what seems radical. Seems is the word, here. It is most often a new religion with a comfortable pew. Because most of them live in a society, or within a section of society where the opposing viewpoint is in disgrace.

Lobbying for a cause is hardly anyone's first choice in life. It can become such after life has failed you in other ways. If you haven't become the glass blower you wanted to be, for instance, find a cause within glass blowing and relate this to the environment.

Take it upon yourself to change the rules by which others may play. And order the game on from the sidelines. You may never have to blow a piece of glass again.

Nor am I trying to reduce the best intentions of those who find hunting cruel. Yet, no more cruel than using a hammer on a calf's skull, or gaffing a struggling tuna to a boat.

And you can make a case that, if the new acceptable fashion was a resurgence of drinking cattle blood, some of those I talked to in Toronto that night would find some way to be morally outraged at those of us who did not do it.

George Orwell, said in his article on PEN International, that the problem with certain rebels against the status quo was that they were most often rebels against a sense of integrity in their own nature. And this is how I cannot help viewing at least some of these people—the fellow from Kingston, Ontario, and his British counterpart, who were as amused with my opinions as they were with someone else's table manners.

It is often viewed by themselves, however, as it was that night, in my case, as a glorious sermonizing to the lesser lights.

So often those who try to attain sainthood leave the salt of the earth behind.

—1993

Driving at Night

For years, I worked at night. Sometimes in the winter I saw nothing more of the sun than a slight glow. I never minded it too much. But wanting to get onto a day schedule caused all kinds of trouble. Generally, no matter how much I tried, I slipped back to my nocturnal habits, boiled a pot of tea at midnight and went to work. For a number of years this caused a problem. If I had to travel from place to place, I couldn't start before the sun was down, because I wouldn't be awake enough to go. Never, when driving through to Ontario from the Miramichi, did I get onto the Plaster Rock highway until after dark.

Sometimes in the winter, I travelled miles without meeting another car, and sometimes without seeing so much as a rabbit.

I don't think you see the world the same way anyway. Or the same things in the world. So often people are by themselves. And as we know from experience, there are few things in Canada that can kill you, but the weather is one.

So you don't like to see people stranded.

There was a young man my wife and I picked up one night who hauled a switchblade on us, his arms tattooed with numbchucks, and his insistence that he had a black belt in karate.

My wife was driving and as he sat behind me, holding the knife against the seat, he kept talking about going home to kick his brother in the head. The bumpy battered road was empty for a long time.

He kept railing on, about some great thing he had lost, someone who had deserted him.

Yet, I think all-in-all, tough boys are like drunkards. The less they say about it, the more you know they're the genuine article. After awhile I told him he had to put his knife away. And he looked at it as if he was recognizing it for the first time, nodded and smiled. For the rest of the trip we talked about country and western music. Both of us were fans.

I don't know where I was coming from one night. But at two in the morning I went around a turn. In the dooryard of a small house was a man, stark naked waving an axe. As if he was limbering up for the local woodsman contest next day.

I saw him later on. In daylight he sat on the broken lawn chair fully dressed and stared benignly at the twisted road between Neguac and Burnt Church. And he's gone from us now. One day he just wasn't there any more.

The house eventually got more and more solitary- and deserted-looking, patched with dried-looking bushes and weeds, and after a time was torn down. I never knew who he was or learned his name. Nothing marks his spot now, except part of a foundation, a grey desolate chimney frame.

Being alone seems to be the thing about night travel. This is what I'm trying to say about it. Not only for myself but for those I've met along the way.

Even when I tried to and planned to daylight drive, I still was on the Plaster Rock at midnight.

Its a better road now then it once was, but still there are miles of what some would call nothing. Trees and darkness. For a long time it wasn't paved.

One time in the late '70s I was travelling there: I saw what I thought was a wounded deer.

It kept moving toward me out of the left darkness. I slowed down, when it walked into the middle of the road and began to wave. He was covered in blood, wearing one shoe and holding the other in his hand, and his tie was twisted completely around. All the buttons of his shirt, except the one under his tie were torn off, showing the friendly stretch marks of an enormous beer gut.

"How are you?" I asked.

"Not so bad—can you help me find my car?"

"Where did you last see it?"

"Somewhere in the ditch."

He should go to the hospital. But as you can guess, this wasn't his idea. His idea was that he would find his car and go home as quickly as he could. And being drunk, he was determined to find it before the cops did.

"It couldn't have sneaked away too, too far," he said hopefully as if to encourage my participation in the search.

But it wasn't anywhere he thought. That is, it wasn't in either ditch, and he had been wandering both sides of the road for a half an hour looking for it.

His car was, we eventually saw, in the woods, about 100 feet from the road, up against a spruce tree.

He had no idea how it got there.

I told him to take the half-dozen broken and unbroken beer and to try to get rid of them. He thought about the best way to do this. And then he offered me one and we leaned against what was left of the hood.

"Weather's nice," he said.

"Pretty good," I said.

"On vacation, are ya?"

"I guess so," I said.

He hadn't remembered anything about going through the air, crossing the 20 foot ditch and sailing into the woods.

He hadn't remembered where he'd been, or where he was going. But what was worse for him, was that he had lost the new teeth his family had gotten him for his birthday.

I suggested he must have lost them in the car, and looked about under the dash for them. A strange kind of invasion of privacy I guess. But he kept searching the ground, swinging his shoe at the grass morosely, until another car pulled over. I did happen to find his teeth near the brake peddle.

And we persuaded him to get in with those who had just stopped, to travel to Grand Falls, the closest hospital to us.

In the dark we were a few spots of light on the edge of nowhere. His hair greying, and his tie, twisted completely about, as if he'd recently attempted to hang himself.

I never saw him again.

There was another night: We were coming back from a wedding. It was after two in the morning. There was one other car in front of us. I told Peggy I couldn't chance to pass him, because I couldn't tell when he might veer into the middle of the road.

He would do 60, and then slow down to 20. He went around turns on the wrong side.

We were about 35 miles from Fredericton when he tried to go around a turn, crossed the center line and went tumbling straight down a 40 foot embankment.

I went walking along the road trying to spot him, and was joined in a minute by a man from New York.

Far down in the turn we could make out a feeble light and the sound of a woman—who I thought was speaking Spanish.

Then we saw them coming up the bank, and we scrambled down to meet them, the woman carrying a baby in her arms. They were from India, and the woman was dressed in traditional Hindu dress. The man was absolutely, painfully sober. A fact he wanted us to know. Though exhausted he hadn't thought of pulling over.

At any rate the young fellow from New York went on his way, and we all walked to my car.

When they got into our back seat, I started to drive to the hospital in Oromocto (we were 15 miles from it).

"No. no," the gentleman said, "We must now go to the police station and make out the report."

The woman spoke to him for a second.

And he spoke angrily back, "But we must make out the report to the police, about my car."

Then they spoke for a few more moments in their language.

The woman told us she had been breast feeding the baby and it fell from her arms when the car went over the embankment.

"And now it doesn't want to wake up anymore," she said.

Everyone was silent. The night smelled sweet. It was in the middle of summer.

"Let me see it—I'll wake it."

The man took the baby from her. And he began to flip it into the air.

In my rearview mirror, I saw the baby (I never found out if it was a boy or girl) being tossed to the car ceiling, hover for a moment, and come tumbling back down. Only to be flipped up again.

"I'll wake it—and then we'll go to the police and make out a decent report," the gentleman said.

We went to the hospital. The nurse got the baby to wake, and then a doctor took it. But I never heard from them again and am not sure what happened to it.

Insanity can happen, drunk or sober, in the company of strangers.

Although, to tell the truth, I much preferred the drunk.

The last two cases involve holding hands:

The first was on a train going through from Halifax to Newcastle some years ago. It was late at night.

The train was almost empty.

The moon shone down over the snow, and the sky looked like a grey chalk board.

"Stop trying to hold my hand," I heard a woman say in back of me.

There had been a little fellow bothering her for some time, although no one knew.

First he walked by and sat with her. Then, when she moved her seat, he followed her—this was when they were behind me, and tried to hold her hand.

And after she told him that she didn't want to hold hands with him, he got up and walked by me.

He was about 25, couldn't have been more than 5' 2", and wore lifts.

The train rocked its way through the woods, and everyone forgot about him.

Ten minutes later the car door banged open and he went flying by me with a conductor chasing him.

"That's him—that's him," a second woman yelled, following the conductor.

"That's him," the first woman said.

And he ran down to the end of the car, as fast as his legs would carry him, as another conductor cut him off. It seemed as if he was trapped to me. I didn't know how he'd get out of it. But never underestimate the value of panic.

"Twack," he hit the conductor, who was trying to block his exit, square in the head, and the conductor staggered and went down.

And then he did, what seemed to me to be absolutely unexpected. He jumped off the train.

We were out looking under the train for him at one in the morning. We did not find him.

"I hope he's not squished," one of the young women said, as the train started up again.

"He's not squished—you would have heard the squish," the other woman said.

The few of us looked out the train windows, into the grey silence.

The last case is similar to the others. Perhaps it is the archetypal case for those who drive at night.

It happened to a friend of mine. At three in the morning—coming back from somewhere. He left the road, and was thrown from his car. He lay in the ditch, his life going from him. No one about.

Until a young woman pulled over. They had never met before.

She told him she would have to go get him help, because it was in the middle of the night, and they were all alone.

"Oh, no," he said, smiling at her for a second, "I'll be okay if you don't leave me. Just hold my hand—and don't let go." She took his hand and held unto it. Those were the last words he spoke.

I know these things aren't unusual or important whatsoever. But the memory of them has been with me for a long time. I have a kinder opinion now of the gentleman with the baby than I once had.

Being under stress he was only trying to do the right thing, not knowing his thinking was muddled. Perhaps new to our country, and conscious of bureaucratic reports he was only frightened of being sent away.

Perhaps too, it's summed up by the man I met on the Plaster Rock, the man with his tie twisted about his neck.

"Thank God you stopped," he said, smiling that wonderfully kind self-depreciating smile so many New Bruswickers have. "Tonight, I'm on my own."

I related some of these stories once to a woman. She told me New Bruswick roads held no surprise for her. But she and her husband travel from one bed and breakfast to the other, and are always off the road by dark.

—1994

Hockey

I don't know what the main unifying linchpin for
Canadian culture is. But I can guess. Recently, on CBC's
The Journal, I was asked that question. And I am sure I
disappointed the interviewer with the answer. I said,
"Hockey." Of course, in deference to the interviewer, I
said, "Ice hockey." But it was never called ice hockey when
I was growing up. That's before the Americans took over
and repackaged it for us. So it became ice hockey. The
Americans didn't invent the term either. They got it from
people they wish to believe know the game better than any
Canadian has a right to—that is, the Europeans.

I don't know if they will run the particular *The Journal*
program I was guest on. The CBC's *The Journal* and I have
a history of getting our wires crossed—which for me I
think is just as well. I suppose if I had said the unifying
linchpin of our national soul was Canada's Foreign Policy
or perhaps its Multiculturalism then I would have fared
better.

But in all honesty I couldn't say that.

One of the people on *The Journal* mentioned Canada's
sense of fairness and diplomacy in External Affairs as
being far more "nation defining" than hockey. So let's
reflect on this for a second.

Canadian External Affairs has used distant places like South Africa as moral whipping posts for years—all the while running from the tremendous overfishing off of our east coast and from a cry for moral support by the Newfoundland fishery. Which certainly showed some lack of moral courage closer to home.

Either way this does not do Canadians credit.

However it does point out the cultural gulf, between myself and those I am sometimes invited to talk to.

It doesn't matter much though. Our main tunnel of political and cultural vision has always seemed to me to be a type of balloon bursting of our own best interests. We have pulled the wool over our own eyes so often that most of us have come to accept the view others have of us. Most of what Canada is or has been is somehow decided by England, France and the U.S.A.—that is, our allies, who believe it is necessary to browbeat us every so often about seals or aboriginal peoples, and at least in a symbolic or psychological way, our hockey, knowing that those of us in Ottawa or Toronto will tend to cringe if somebody in London or Washington or Paris does not like us.

The Irish playwright and boozing pug—whose work I like—Brendan Behan, ridiculed us in 1957: "Canada should stick to it's league—ice hockey."

But it's too bad we didn't take his advice.

I suppose it doesn't matter. The Skydome is now a national sports treasure and baseball is becoming the sport of choice. It has been our ideal to link ourselves with the United States, so we can have the same kind of fun they do.

We even might think it's an even playing ground—that Toronto having a baseball franchise is just like Los Angeles having a hockey one.

Our whole idea of entertainment and fun tends to come from Hollywood—and for 60 years the movies habitually have taught us two things—you can't have fun where it snows—and where the temperature is subzero people must be humorless and unsophisticated. We continually apologize for our weather, and tend to want the ideas of fun manufactured in New York and Miami.

So we have given the greatest game in the world away fearing that if we dominate it ourselves it can't be good. I'm sure the gurus of national culture would much rather we all play soccer.

The president of the National Hockey League is American and the head office is now in New York City.

However it is not only John Zeagler, (1990) president of the NHL, who wants Americans to think that Americans, not Canadians, play the game of hockey. The underlying intention of most NHL policy is to make it seem that way.

Canadians wittingly or unwittingly partake in this contrivance of truth for benefits that have always remained obscure to me. By loosening the reins on our own national sport the last thing we have to do is stand tall in any saddle.

Canada has practice enough to know that the ultimate deceit is the one which we so readily use against ourselves.

A franchise in El Paso becomes, in Zeagler's mind, good for the game, while one in Saskatoon does not.

But so often what is touted as "good for the game" by John Zeagler, and recently by Wayne Gretzky, is ultimately bad for Canada.

The startling observation I've had is that the more things happen that are good for the game—the less Canadians, who know the game in their soul better than any other people alive, care about it.

Everything is done to make it seem like hockey is just baseball or football on a slippery surface. Home colours have changed—so I still, for a second, think Montreal is playing at home when they are in Chicago, or Chicago is at home when they are in Toronto. That is, the home colours are white—just as in baseball.

Players are announced before a big game—the starting line up, like in football. Parody has become essential for the gate—the season now runs into May (1990). People pay their dues at the US college hockey level—just as in football.

Ninety percent of the Maine Bears—which were number one in the States two years ago—are Canadian. I have a clipping from a paper where Maine scored five goals against some western college team. All of these goals were scored by a Canadian player.

It is essentially the same for our women. Most of the best are gone to the States, and won the first World Women's Hockey Championship as—you guessed it—a pick-up team.

But worse, the essential nature of the game is being manipulated off the ice. Our public opinion makers or at least a certain segment of the entrenched middle class believe that Canadian hockey is violent. And react against it, as if they are reacting against American chauvinism. (These are the same people who now watch baseball). Canadian hockey is violent. Not Soviet hockey or Swedish hockey, or Finnish Hockey. But Canadian hockey. Each referee in an international tournament can exploit this belief at his will, not because he is unfair but because it is a learned response from the crowd that he himself believes.

That is they know they have the court of world opinion on their side. It has not gotten better since 1972—when in the last game against the Soviets we played over half the game short-handed and won. It has gotten worse. (It is also interesting to note that in one of the glossy hardbacks about the history of our game Team Canada of 1972 is called "Team NHL" What Canadian would allow this to happen? Well, in the media I've come to expect anything.) Hockey to me is emblematic of the problems our nation has in exercising our moral courage. I've spoken of this before.

On a radio program in Maine in 1987, I mentioned that our most famous hockey stars played in the U.S.—and could be considered by Americans to be Americans as well—the radio talk show host assumed ALL of them were Americans.

The Canada Cup is not really a showcase for our sport—no matter how much we want and pretend it to be one. It is played in September—and although the Soviets practise for months to prepare for it and though Larianov admitted to a Swedish paper after their defeat in 1987 that to them nothing matters more than beating Canada the Soviets themselves don't officially recognize it as a world tournament.

There are always aspersions cast against it. Of course, by the Europeans. But I wonder how many know that the president of the NHL probably hates the concept of it—for it shows that the best hockey players in the NHL are still Canadians. I've never seen a man so worried that he is showing his true face, as John Zeagler during the Canada Cup.

Finally, its importance is trivialized by the magazine that has become the vehicle for promoting the NHL in the United States, and as a by-product of this promotion, Soviets into the League—*Sports Illustrated*. They openly dismissed Team Canada in 1987.

They did it by smugly linking falsehood with truth. They suggested that Team Canada was nothing without Gretzky or Lemieux—by this reckoning all Soviet players were better than all the other players on Team Canada.

Canadians don't have a magazine of their own; and if by off-chance they did then no one outside of Canada would ever see it. But that aside, if the American owners cannot make the sport American then they will continue to make it international. If it's not their game it won't be ours.

Let me ask a question: If a Swede and a boy from Bellefond, New Brunswick, of similar talent were up for grabs in L.A., who do you think would be taping up his stick in L.A.? And who would be slogging it out on buses in the American Hockey League?

Public ignorance will allow for misinformation on television as well as in *Sports Illustrated*.

Our broadcasters generally, at least those schooled like most CBC sports announcers, pretend not to notice insults and indifference directed at the contribution Canada has made to the sport.

Why must we pretend that the Americans like us and are promoting "our" game. Listen to Mike Erusioni during the Olympics. Why must we be coerced into believing that an American television audience is essential to the wellbeing of hockey. It's lasted okay for 80 years.

And, thirdly, why do we mistake moral cowardice for civility, and so continually mince statements and willingly blindside ourselves to what is being said, or not said about Canada elsewhere.

Witness Ken Dryden as a commentator on ABC's coverage of the Calgary Olympics in 1988. While two American announcers bemoaned the fact that if only "their" players were released from the NHL the United States would win gold, Dryden, to his shame and Canada's, said very little to dispute them.

We should understand that falsehood never cares at all if it is false. It needs someone to expose it as such. Dryden had the chance to emphatically state Canada's position.

The World Hockey Championships of 1990 was once again the classic showcase for our two nemesises: Soviet players, and Swedish referees. Both want to prove to a watching world that their game is more "moral" than ours.

The Russians and Swedes aren't handcuffed by the thought of the penalty box when the puck is dropped, but they know the Canadians are. The World Hockey Championships don't often seem to be played in Regina.

All in all we fly the flag of the sucker. The sport is lost not because of our international opposition, but because of our national nature to allow others to dictate to us the premise on which we view ourselves.

Our game is, more than most things I can put my finger on, fundamental to the spiritual nature of Canada. The most shining public example of our life as Canadians is not found with the National Ballet but with the more moving, more perfect ballet of Izerman, Gretzky and Lemieux.

All of whose careers have taken them to the States.

If we don't understand this about our hockey three-quarters the rest of the world understand it about their soccer. I think that if Brazil had to beg Peru to release its players for the World Cup soccer championships there would be riots in San Paulo. We can bet they would consider it a national disgrace. And no one in the world would blame them.

—1990

*   *   *

(Since I wrote this essay, Canada has won three more World Junior Men's Hockey Championships, another Canada Cup, a second World Women's Hockey Championship, two Olympic hockey silver medals, and have finally regained the World Hockey Championship. Our country, of course, is still divided on where the nature of our identifying spirit lies.)

Some Thoughts on Weather

Half the summer I waited for them to arrive, because their travel dates weren't firm—my good friends from the South. And you know the one thing I worried about—the weather.

Now I know and you know that the weather here is wonderful—it's just that "they" don't know. "They" never find out. "They" never seem to be here when it's great.

They make lots of fun of our weather. I've heard them. Even in Maine. And one can make a case that if New Bruswick is, (how do we say it in the new correct language)—socially challenged—it is because we're joined at the hip to a state that's been in a continual grip of narcolepsy since 1821.

Once, in Calais, they asked a group of kids on the street what St. Stephen was like.

"Oh, it is cold way over there"

And when I gave a reading in New Orleans and was invited to a house in the French Quarter for dinner, a woman said to me:

"Why, I hear it's all so cold in Canada that you can't bury your dead in the winter—is that all true?"

"Why, that's all true," a man said. "Why, I all collected a wolverine skull up there—you all wanta see my wolverine bones?"

"But aren't your graves sinking down here?" I said.

"Why, that's just such an ungracious stereotype about our graves sinking—and from a Canadian, too—how all did you ever even hear of it way up there?"

"The Tragically Hip."

We must remember though that when we look at a map—we are up there. There aren't too too many places farther up there than we are. I mean when you go farther up there, where do you go? Sometimes when you travel and tell people where you live they will look at you, blinking with the rather complicated expression of someone who has just been hit in the face with a snow shovel.

"Where you say you are?"

"New Brunswick."

"New—"

"Brunswick."

"Oh, Brunswick—"

"Nooo—New Brunswick."

"I see—that'd be in Pennsylvania?"

"No, that'd be in New Brunswick—"

"Ohh—I see!" (The shifting of gears on an automatic transmission. The dead silence.) "Where you say you are?"

It takes a John Wayne kind of man not to feel apologetic over it. A kind of man that can say:

"Yes, ma'am, I do come from a small place—an isolated place, as you say—where we can't all bury our dead in the winter—but, ma'am, people up there are honest and hard working—well, honest—well, there are still people up there, ma'am—so, I think it just better if I leave."

"Where did that almost quiet stranger with the funny accent all say he was from?"

But I must remember that once out of Canada, nine-tenths of the people I've met have hardly ever seen snow. A flake here and there, to be sure, some of them, but not 14-feet up against your back window for months on end. They just cannot comprehend it—and along with it goes their idea of backward isolation. If there's a white-out on the highway, people like us are probably forced to stay at home and eat the sled dog.

Snow sets a panic in people from other climes.

When I was Writer-in-Residence in Virginia a few winters back, there was a disturbing dusting of snow, one night. An inch or two up on the Blue Ridge. The next morning, I went to the cafeteria for breakfast wearing sneakers and a jean jacket and met a dozen people with face toques on, treking along between the Administrative Building and the English Department, as if they were engaged in a strange experiment most of them were bound to fail.

"Hello," some managed.

"How she goin' right there now?" I said.

A child of about three, piggybacked on his mother, looked at me as if I was going in the wrong direction—the direction that everyone else was trying to escape. I trudged on to get my cappuccino and great big hot cross bun.

"We're all closed," a woman told me, almost in hysterics, "and I'm tryin to get home. I don't know if Roy can get in to get me out."

"Why?"

"Why? Sir—The storm—For God's sake—The storm—You're the Canadian boy, aren't you?"

"Yes, Ma'am—"

"Well, how unfortunate for you."

Somehow when people mention our weather we all start to smile like Alfred E. Newman in *Mad Magazine*—or like a half a dozen or more of our television announcers have for years.

There is such an irrational quality to everything in Canada, our weather simply fits the bill. Read these, and see the cute little Alfred E. Newman smile:

> "Canada has finally gotten tough with foreign overfishing off the Grand Banks, and has decided to arrest its own vessels."

> "*Live at 5* will profile the rise to the top of ATV's own—Oprah Winfrey."

> "We have a world-renowned World War One great flying ace—Why not make a documentary and call him a bald-faced liar."

> "Lucien Bouchard."

I mean why complain about snow.

My friends were arriving from the South. I couldn't tell if it was sleet or snow that was being swept in off the bay. It was July 18th.

I took a mat outside to shake, and found myself swinging it furiously up and down to disperse the fog over my barbecue.

And, of course, it didn't let up and it didn't get any better.

"It was so nice last week—LAST week was the week to come—we had—oh, it was almost, I'd say, up around, just about 90 last week—" I told Tasha.

She had just arrived from Mississippi with her dad, this young African-American woman who had not been north since she was a toddler. Whose poetry reflects life in the Deep South. Who writes of summer days so humid you can taste it on the page.

"I just read your new book," she said, "I could just taste the snow off the page."

"Snow—yes but—well, we almost, I mean, from about like June until maybe—oh—sometimes as late as December we don't see a scratch of snow at all—ha ha ha ha ha ha."

She watched me barbecue the steaks and the smoke curled up in the great billows of fog about me.

She had folded her arms, and was shivering under the jacket I had given her, but was too polite to leave me outside alone. Shivering like that she reminded me of the Mark Twain line:

"The coldest winter I ever had was the summer I spent in San Francisco."

"Is that a garden you have?" she said peering into the darkness.

"A garden—yes, of course I have one—a garden, of course, ha ha ha ha ha ha—Come and see it."

We squished along through the grass—it was lying down so flat and soppy I figured I could get away the whole summer without mowing it. It was kind of like grass that you had piled the Brylcream to. My back garage door, banging in the scowling wind, looking like it had been overcome by woodrot.

The carrots were up about one-eighth of an inch. I plucked them a bit, not to pull them out of the ground, but to make them look bigger. Fused with the one tomato, and finally grabbed a radish.

"Wanta eat a radish?" I said, thrusting it into her face.

"Oh, no thanks," she smiled.

"Some good," I said, trying to chew it, and spitting it, somewhat like pieces of a rubber ball, out of my mouth little by little as I walked behind her to the deck.

Her father, Rick, grew up in Canada. "Daddy says when he was young the river froze and he could skate on it."

I realized she was asking me this to see if it was true. That to her it was almost incomprehensible.

"That's true."

"Really—he could skate on the river?"

"Of course."

And then I remembered a man I know from Nigeria, who wrote home to his parents, the first January he was at university in Fredericton, and told them he had just been walking on water. They wrote back, telling him they were worried that he was suffering from delusions of grandeur and asked him to come home.

In Brisbane, Australia, last fall, we met a woman who had to come to Canada in January. She was frightened that the weather would get her. It was an abnormal fear that made her question whether or not she should come.

"What's the temperature in January?" She asked me.

"Pardon me now?"

"The temperature?"

"My, this fish—what did you say this fish is -60—called?" The truth will set you free. It sets you free, if you tell it—rarely, if you hear it.

The woman reminded me of the poor soul in the Checkov story, who while in the sick bay on a ship kept trying to be reassured that they wouldn't hit a fish and sink.

"And, if there's a storm, they'll be able to get to my house—and rescue me."

"Why, no, Ma'am—not after -40—cause the traffic dies, and no one can get on the road after that. Cold does somethin' to a man—I don't know—it eats at his soul— changes him. After -40, people change."

There is a way to play along with all of it—as the Aussies do with their white sharks. Because what people believe proves, finally, what they don't know. And, of course, if there is a bad storm, we're much safer in Canada where we've learned what to do. I mean, we've figured out INSULATION.

We had a wonderful dinner with Tasha and Rick but the weather didn't change. It got worse. It seemed that everything fell except snow.

"It was—it was—It was great here last week—"

But it was pointless. It was not that Tasha didn't want to believe. It was simply the body of evidence. Days and days of rain. I'm telling you, she spent eight days in the Maritimes and didn't see the sun.

"It's just an unfortunate bad stretch," I said. And then I began to explain how the weather is sometimes like a giant elastic that keeps stretching—and the longer it stretches, the more painful it's bound to be when it snaps.

I don't know if Tasha took any solace in my lies or not. I hope so because I like her a great deal.

But there is something about our weather. It's like the man who finds the singing frog, who will sing only for him. Everytime he goes to show it off it simply goes "RIBIT." Everyone laughs and goes away.

But how beautiful its voice when alone.

How beautiful our land is to us.

—1993

Travel

Someone once said that the quickest way out of Glasgow was a bottle of Bols gin. Well, I know people who have proved this all their lives with Captain Morgan rum. They never had to leave the room where they drank to travel on every ship that left the Miramichi. Fight in every battle.

As Owen Feltham said in the 17th century: Fancy gives you wings to fly. So at times, does cheap booze.

It can be argued, also, that we never go anywhere without bringing along what we most want to leave behind—namely, ourselves. I have found this true enough on more than one occasion. Therefore, we can say, with some measure of certainty, that we never do go anywhere. That where we are is as close to the centre of the universe as we are bound to get.

There is a Arabic saying that travel is a foretaste of hell. And when that line was first uttered they still had the luxury of travelling by camel.

What might they say if they had to travel across the International Dateline, ending up in a small hotel room with a three-year-old child singing the theme song from *Barney* at one o'clock in the morning:

> "I love you—you love me—
> We're a happy family—"

But I have travelled enough to know one thing: I can't stop now. And though the information I have stored up over the years has told me time and again—something like regularly being hit over the head with a snow shovel—that it just isn't worth it, I'm sure I'll be on the road again in a month or two.

These are a few travel experiences I've had so far.

I hit a hurricane off the coast of Africa when I was 20, on a banana boat. I was a 3rd class passenger, and there was one liferaft for 35 of us—not that any of us would have been stupid enough to get into it. There were four life boats for the four first class passengers—one life boat per person—and two life boats for the eight second class passengers. We had one. We were all shoved into the stern of the ship like mice—thirty-two African students, my brother, myself, and a cockney boy from London. Almost everyone was seasick. All except myself and the cockney boy—and, to tell the truth, I don't know why we weren't either.

At the height of the storm—when our Spanish captain was required to show nerves of steel, he was busy screaming his head off and telling the First Mate he would pitch him overboard. Running about with tiny tears in his eyes and laughing at the silliest things.

I've been stuck in the Kootenay's in mid-winter, and they are fine people, but, to tell the truth, I wanted to be home.

"My God, we've got you here now," my guest said, with some surprise and wonderment, the very moment I arrived. "But with this storm coming in over the mountains, can't you smell it? God knows when we'll get you out—no one hardly ever comes here in the winter, and we never thought you would: better just make the best of it. How was your plane ride?"

"A little bumpy."

"Last plane came in—everyone puked!"

I've been stuck on the tarmac in Baltimore for five hours, in Dorval Airport for seven, and in Heathrow in London for almost three days snitching leftover crackers from restaurant tables.

In Baltimore I had to keep convincing this little old lady, who would wake up periodically, that not only hadn't we landed, we hadn't as yet left the ground.

Once, on a particularly rough flight, from somewhere to somewhere else in the middle of the night, the only thing I could hear—and it was, I believe, the last thing I would hear, was this little girl about seven—all I could see was her pigtails sticking straight up in the air, tied in bows with two pink ribbons—shouting at the top of her lungs:

"MOMMIE MOMMIE—MOMMIE MOMMIE MOMMIE—MOMMIE MOMMIE."

"Someone do the decent thing and slap her," I almost shouted, and then decided I better not.

On Quantas flights over the Pacific, they have a screen set up which keeps feeding you information, while showing the image of a tiny vulnerable plane inching across the ocean.

"YOU ARE NOW 4 THOUSAND KM FROM YOUR POINT OF DEPARTURE, AT 38,000 FEET."

"YOU ARE NOW 4 THOUSAND AND 20 KM FROM YOUR POINT OF DEPARTURE, AT 36,000 FEET."

"YOU ARE NOW 4 THOUSAND AND 92 KM FROM YOUR POINT OF DEPARTURE, AT 35,643 FEET."

It's a maddening experience, and after a while the man behind me started muttering (I'm sure he didn't think I heard);

"Alright, alright—just keep it in the air."

There is one good thing about all this—you can continually make up new blurbs for book covers for yourself, which although not lies, have almost nothing to do with the truth. Things like:

"Tossed by hurricanes off the coast of Africa; Storm stuck in the Kootenay's, and Braved SHARK INFESTED water off the coast of Australia," or something like that.

If you aren't able to leave yourself behind when you travel, you are at least able to take more of yourself with you, the further you get from home.

For instance, I come from the rocks in Newcastle, N.B., CANADA. I come from the rocks. They aren't really big—and, really, I don't know where they are, because I've never seen them).

But once I leave Newcastle to go anywhere else on the Miramichi, I am known as a Newcastler.

Once off the Miramichi, I become a Miramicher.

In the Maritimes, I am a New Brunswicker.

In Canada, I am a Maritimer.

In Australia, or any place else, I am a Canadian (once I tell them I'm not American, which I usually do, unless I have just finished making an idiot of myself.)

The upshot of it all is this: If I really travel enough I might someday finally become a recognized citizen of the world. Which won't make travelling any less fun than it already is.

—1994

About the Author

David Adams Richards was born in Newcastle, New Brunswick, in 1950. His first novel, *The Coming of Winter*, won the Norma Epstine Prize in 1974, and and appeared in translation in the Soviet Union. His other novels are *Blood Ties*, *Lives of Short Duration*, *Road to the Stilt House*, *Nights Below Station Street* (winner of the 1988 Governor General's Award for Fiction); *Evening Snow Will Bring Such Peace* (winner of the 1990 Canadian Authors Association Award). His latest novel, *For Those Who Hunt the Wounded Down*, was shortlisted for the 1993 Governor General's Award for Fiction, and won the 1994 Atlantic Provinces Booksellers Award. Richards has also received the 1993 Canada-Australia Prize, and the 1993/1994 Alden Nowlan Award for Excellence in English Literary Arts in New Brunswick.

In 1986, Richards was named one of Canada's Ten Best Fiction Writers in the "45 Below" Competition. He also received an award from *Maclean's* magazine as one of 12 Canadians they recognized whose accomplishments "made a difference" in 1989. Richards has also written several original screenplays including "Small Gifts" which was made into a film and aired on CBC in 1993.

David Adams Richards lives in Saint John, New Brunswick, with his wife, Peggy, and their son, John Thomas.

Selected Publications

Broken Jaw Chapbooks
Salvador, A.J. Perry
Drawings by Poet, Beth Jankola
Hawthorn, Arthur Bull; Ruth Bull (illustrator)

Broken Jaw Press
Chaste Wood, karl wendt
Dark Seasons, Georg Trakl; Robin Skelton (translator)
Poems for Little Cataraqui, Eric Folsom
A Lad From Brantford & other essays, David Adams Richards
voir dire, pj flaming (NEW MUSE 1994 Award winner)

New Muse of Contempt
A semi-annual international magazine of mail art and
literary writing–poetry, visual poetry, fiction, essays, and
reviews–edited and published since 1987 by Joe Blades.
$7/year   ISSN 0840-4747

For a full catalogue, please send a SASE to:
M•A•P•PRODUCTIONS
BOX 596 STN A   SAN 1171437
FREDERICTON NB E3B 5A6
CANADA

imprimerie gagné ltée

PRINTED IN CANADA